Clear

How to Simplify Your Life and Live More Fearlessly

ANNICK MAGAC

*May this book help
you get "clear"!*

Pour Maman et Papa, who have taught me
what it means to have a home.

CONTENTS

Clear

How to Simplify Your Life
and Live More Fearlessly

Preface

The idea for this book has been in incubation for more than 18 years. It all started with my journey to design school for college. Or, perhaps it was even earlier when I was a child obsessed with visiting old mansions and monuments, which I still love to do today. I probably can also tie it to the psychic I visited, uncharacteristically, on a whim in the East Village of New York, with a friend in 1996. The psychic ceremoniously told me I would write a book someday.

Clear: How to Simplify Your Life and Live More Fearlessly is a culmination of my passions: Design, Health, and Mindset--all of which I have spent many years studying and practicing. When I first started my career in NYC working as an interior designer, I had no idea I would help people with their homes but also with their lives. When people invite you behind their closed doors, they let you into a part of their lives that others rarely see. In the comfort of their homes, people would open up in ways that continually surprised me. I found that, along with the design work I was hired to do, I spent a lot of time listening to my clients talk about their lives and relationships.

In retrospect, it isn't much of a shock that I eventually transitioned into health coaching. When I started to coach clients, people would come to me with health concerns related to diet and exercise. As we started to dig beneath the surface of their concerns and work on their mindset to see why they were having issues and how we could develop a program to make sustainable changes, I would ask them about their home and work environments. Inevitably, they would be unhappy with some aspect of their surroundings, but never thought of it as an issue that might be linked to other areas of their lives. I was able to use my unique design background and experience to see things in their home that they couldn't see themselves. One such example is a client, Haley, who was single and hated sleeping in her bedroom. Hung in view from her bed was a beloved painting of an empty rowboat adrift in a cold ocean. I pointed out that she might currently feel like that rowboat and that she might want to consider a warmer, inviting scene to welcome love and partnership into her life. She immediately made that as intention and the painting was hastily relocated into another room. Within months, she was in a wonderful relationship. After many years of observing this, I came to the conclusion that *your surroundings are a reflection of your life.*

When I incorporated work on augmenting habitats into a coaching program, I began to see more substantial life changes happening within a shorter amount of time. Not only did those clients feel better physically and mentally, they felt more joy and ease in the environments they occupied daily, which led to more overall happiness.

Through health coaching and personal space redesign, I have helped clients release old, limiting habits and thought patterns. This process has helped people overcome fear-based thoughts, develop healthy surroundings filled with beauty, and become more successful.

In order to change, we must change the way we do things or *live*. This book will provide you with insights, tips and exercises that will make you think about how your surroundings are a reflection of your current life. It will also offer tried-and-true guided actions on how to change your surroundings to obtain the life that you want. There will be parts of this process that are so liberating you will ask yourself, "Why didn't I do this years ago?" The action steps outlined within these pages will require introspection and work. With respect to your busy lifestyle, the exercises are designed to take as little time as possible. You may find that certain exercises resonate with you. Spend more time on the ones you like and as little as you want on the others.

Throughout *Clear*, I ask that you keep an open mind and an open heart. When we allow new ideas and ways of living into our lives, the changes can be profound.

Now, let's get started.

Introduction

I grew up in the suburbs in a typical American-style raised ranch. It was a pale sage color with black shutters that accented the windows. An enormous pine tree that stood guard in the front yard. While all the houses in the neighborhood looked more or less the same on the outside--such was the style at the time--ours was completely different on the inside. Besides the cooking smells being completely different--try a savory red wine soaked boeuf bourguignon instead of boiled hot dogs and boxed mac n cheese--our house was void of the recliners, Laura Ashley fabrics, and faux wood furniture typical of most homes at the time. Instead, my French immigrant parents had floor-to-ceiling damask window treatments, French provincial style furniture, and real artwork on the walls.

My mother came from a generation that believed in keeping a house so ours was always clean and organized. If anything was broken, my father immediately fixed it. The yard was always tidy. Windows were cleaned twice a year. Everything that could be ironed was ironed, including the pillowcases. Every single thing had its place. My parents always took great pride in having a beautiful home. They also didn't over think it. It was just how they lived and continue to live today. Aside from keeping a tidy home, my parents also believed in filling the refrigerator with fresh, home-cooked food. Often, that food included fresh vegetables that were grown from the garden in the back yard. Keep in mind homesteading was not in fashion at the time.

As a child, I knew our family was different. When I brought kids over to my house, they always made comments on how weird everything was. "Why do you eat that? Where are the soda and chips? Why does your house look different? Why do your parents speak funny?" were typical questions I was asked. The weird thing is, this never bothered me. With a name like Annick, you accept certain things in life.

My parents liked to visit old mansions and gardens while on vacation. Unlike many kids my age, I loved it! I remember being 10 years old and visiting Franklin D. Roosevelt's house in Hyde Park, NY. I was completely enthralled and hung onto every single word the docent said. The entire experience was sublime. I loved the architecture, design, art, history, and the feeling I had inside that old mansion. I began to recognize that beauty was an important element in those homes we visited and in my own home growing up. Later, it would become apparent how my childhood informed my interests in design, art, and how both affect health--and vice versa.

I guess it should be no surprise that I ended up in NYC at Parsons School of Design for college. I graduated as a Product Designer with a concentration in Furniture Design. Upon graduating, I was recruited--due to my senior thesis project--to work for a prominent architectural firm in their interiors department. I quickly became successful as a designer and was the recipient of a prestigious award for Best of Furniture Design in the I.D. Annual Design Review. It is a yearly contest for the crème de la crème of creative design professionals. From there, I continued my career by working within the interiors world as a designer and consultant. While I was financially fulfilled, there was one big problem: I felt emotionally empty.

The fast-paced New York lifestyle had taken its toll. Despite the incredible experiences of working with top designers, celebrities, and being endlessly inspired by the bustling streets, I couldn't get out of my own way. I felt like I was no good; I ate terribly, drank too much, and the greatest irony of all--I had very little furniture in my apartment.

Yes, you read that correctly. I was a furniture designer without much furniture. The few pieces I had included a chaise I had designed and made; an inherited cheap college-style trunk; two Saarinen tulip chairs I received as payment for babysitting a wretched brat; a folding card table; and a blow-up mattress on the floor that would lose air through the night. I distinctly remember having a potential suitor come over and ask "Did you just move in?" I can still remember the look on his face when I told him I'd lived there for a few years. That was the last time I saw him. At the time, I had no idea that my home reflected what a mess my life was.

Several years later I transitioned completely out of the creative field and took a loathsome sales job in corporate America. I was overweight, still depressed, and my home was in complete disarray. I was at my rock bottom. I felt unfilled with the work I was doing and my personal relationships were strained. I felt constantly angry and blamed everyone, except myself, for my problems. I blamed my boss for hating my job, but I wouldn't leave it. I blamed my weight on traveling for work, but I wouldn't take care of myself. I blamed my partner for all our issues. I blamed the hours I worked on not being able to do anything creative, but I wouldn't change my schedule. I had a thousand excuses for every suggestion someone would give me when I complained, which was all the time. Frankly, I was a horribly negative bore to be around. It shouldn't have come as a surprise that one day when I came home from a week of travel for work, my partner said he was leaving.

I never even saw it coming because I was so preoccupied with myself and my pity party. I was completely stunned and I took it hard. A couple weeks after he moved out, when I was finally in the silence of my home alone, I woke up one day and thought enough is enough. Things have got to change. Whatever I was currently doing was clearly not working. All my decisions and views over the past several years had gotten me as far away from all things and people that I loved that I could get. I knew, deep in my heart, that what was really needed was for *me* to change. I had to stop looking for other people to fix my problems. I had to stop blaming other people for my misery.

I needed to stop living from a place of fear. That was the hardest thing to admit, because fear equaled weakness in my mind. I always took great pride in being emotionally strong and showing a tough face, even if I felt awful inside. While that can get you far in life, it can also wreak havoc on your mind and actions. Any sort of perceived weakness equaled failure to me, so I did nothing for years because I didn't want to fail. I didn't want anyone to see that I was struggling. I feared having anyone know what was going on in my life and how unhappy I was. I knew in my heart that I could only heal if I could finally admit that I needed help. Once I made that decision, I started a quest to face my fears and move toward living fearlessly.

The first thing I did to face my fear of weakness was to seek the guidance of a therapist and a personal trainer. I had always been into fitness and would go through bouts of working out a lot and then not at all. Throughout my life, I had always enjoyed weightlifting and started up again. I was so out of shape at that time, I could barely lift 3-pound weights. As my body grew stronger, so did my mind. I started to focus on changing the way I thought. At the same time, I also grew interested in helping others so I became a NASM-Certified Personal Trainer.

Though I had learned how to strengthen my body, I knew I lacked quality nutrition. I ate horribly. I consumed plenty of sugar and moonlighted as a cake maker for fun. Despite being raised on them, "vegetables" had become a dirty word to me. When I started to clean up my diet and stopped making cakes, I really started to see changes in my life--not only in my body composition but also in my mindset and moods. This experience motivated me to study nutrition and I would become certified by IIN (Institute For Integrative Nutrition) as a Holistic Health Coach. This particular approach to coaching made sense to me because--as I had experienced in my own life--only true healing and change can come from the combination of nutrition, mind, and body.

Once I started to coach clients, a funny thing happened. In addition to helping them with their nutrition, bodies, and mindset, I also worked with them on their homes. Remember that part about me being a furniture/interior designer? Throughout the years, I had always consulted on interiors even when I worked my corporate job.

Although I thought I had hung up my hat, friends and family continued to call for design advice. Secretly, I loved it. It will always be one of the primary passions in my life. Naturally through the coaching, all of my life experiences came together. I found that I was able to help my clients in a unique way. As I worked with clients on their homes and workspaces, I started to see changes in them much more quickly.

Most people are under the impression that they will hire a health coach to help them lose weight or get into shape. It always becomes much more than that. It is impossible to treat one area, such as weight loss, without treating all areas to create real, sustainable change. It is well known that most people who go on crash diets end up gaining more weight back afterwards than they lost on the diet. This happens because they never deal with all the other things in their lives that drive them to overeat.

In working with clients, I realized that our personal surroundings reflect what is going on in our lives. Those surroundings often become roadblocks to growth and self-improvement. This is easy to overlook because the signs can be subtle or we just aren't aware of it. For example, when we unconsciously have a frown on our face when we're thinking a sad thought. If you have a day where you feel unhappy or overwhelmed, it will show up around you. Is your work desk a mess? Do you constantly misplace items, or find yourself late on deadlines or fighting with coworkers? This could be a sign that you hate your job. Or, is your desk perfect, but you have a very dirty and messy car? Maybe your car looks perfect on the outside, but if you opened up the trunk you would see all sorts of odd stuff and garbage rolling around. All the jumbled up feelings and experiences we have in our lives come out in our habitats through clutter, disorganization, and ugliness. Our goal is to have our environments be a positive reflection of our health and wellbeing.

My clients tend to be highly motivated individuals--executives, entrepreneurs and creatives--who have found that during their pursuits they just got a little off track with the big picture. I help these clients by guiding them to create a life that is balanced between their work, personal life, and health. One of the areas I focus on is the environment in which that individual spends time. I have found that personal and professional space can help or hinder long-term improvement. I get them to a place where they feel fulfilled and empowered to be their best self by living fearlessly, which in the end makes them even more successful in their pursuits.

This book is designed to coach and guide you on how to align your environment to what you want out of life so that you can be more successful, live fearlessly and surround yourself with beauty. It is an outline of my concepts and how I work with clients. You don't have to be an executive to get something out of this book. You just need to keep an open mind, be willing to change, and ready to embrace beauty into your life.

ANNICK MAGAC

Part One

Habitat & Habit

One
Product of Our Environment

Our surroundings are a reflection of our lives. Right now, as you read this book you might be seated in a café drinking an Americano or standing in an over crowded subway car. Perhaps you're listening to *Clear* while you drive to work. What got you to where you are right now in this one moment and are you happy with the way your life is right now? As we go through our journey of life, we have many different experiences that play out against numerous backdrops. Wouldn't it be nice to be able to choose what that backdrop looks like and what it says about your life, while also learning how to live fearlessly?

Through *Clear*, you will see how your environment is formed and a reflection of your life, how to take control of your habitat and move from being overwhelmed to empowered. You will also learn how to beautify your surroundings so as to lead you to be more successful in your life. At the end of each chapter, you will find exercises or lessons that will lead you on how to take the concepts from *Clear* and translate them into changing your mindset and helping you actively beautify your surroundings to live more fearlessly.

৵৯

As we begin this journey, the first place to start is to understand how our habitats and habits are developed from our childhood to how we currently live and think. Are we a product of our environment or is our environment a product of us?

Bruce grew up in an old industrial New England town where everyone knew each other a little too well. He spent most of his time with his grandmother and grandfather while his divorced mother worked the third shift at the local factory and waitressed on the weekends to make enough money to support Bruce, his younger brother, and aging parents. His Mother had moved back into her parents' house when Bruce was three and his brother was a baby when his Father left the family and moved to Montana with his new girlfriend. Growing up in the small town, everyone knew his family, their story, and had their own expectations for how the boys would turn out as adults. Most people were born and raised in the town without ever leaving. People typically got married right out of school, started families young, and worked in the local factories or businesses.

Because there were so many people living in the small house, Bruce and his brother shared a tiny bedroom on the third floor with one window that looked directly into a neighboring house. All the furniture in the room, which wasn't much due to the size, was a hand-me-down from townsfolk or an old piece that was repurposed from another area of the old house. As the boys grew into teenagers the tiny bedroom became stifling, as the two became too big to fit into the space together.

Although the house was warm and loving, Bruce could not wait to get into college and leave his small town behind. He loved his family, but he felt suppressed by the small town mentality and hated that people perceived him as being from the poor family. For college, he ended up in Texas where he stayed as an adult to pursue his career in the oil and gas industry. As soon as he was able to, he bought the biggest house he could afford in the outer most area of his town. Bruce wanted space and he wanted anonymity.

While the house fulfilled Bruce's criteria for what he wanted and how he envisioned he should live, he was lacking in other areas of his life. He was drastically overweight, single, and a self-proclaimed workaholic without ever feeling like he was getting ahead in his career. He rarely ate at home because he hated to eat alone. Every night he worked late, had dinner in town, and drank a few too many cocktails. He would later drive home and pass out on his brand new furniture. He was not happy with his life and he didn't know where to begin to start to change.

Bruce had made every decision in his adult life based on trying to create the opposite experience he had as a child. Because he hated to share the small room with his brother, living in a small town, and feeling poor, he tried to build a house that felt expansive, secluded, and rich. The problem is that he didn't know how to make it warm, safe, and filled with love, the very things his family had provided for him without him being aware of it. It wasn't until he started to work through his issues and getting healthy that he realized he had created a habitat that wasn't reflective of what he wanted, but instead a creation of what he feared. Once Bruce defined what he wanted out of life- a loving family, financial freedom, and great health- he was able to change his environments to support those decisions and go from feeling overwhelmed and frustrated to empowered and successful.

With the way we live our lives, as adults, we can reflect back to different parts of our lives that have influenced how we look at or do things currently. We can all recall a home that we lived in throughout our lives that may have shaped how we viewed the world or decided was how *home* should be, or be influenced by a role model.

Sometimes, How you set up your home has a lot to do with the physical environment in which you live. I once visited my friend, Andy who has an apartment on the lower east side of New York City. Andy is part mad scientist, engineer, and artist who is so smart that half the time you can't even follow him on what he is conceptually talking about. Andy has lived in the same 300 square foot apartment since the mid-sixties. As a designer, he has accumulated an enormous amount of parts and material from more than 40 years of working on projects. The amazing thing is that he has designed his apartment to fit him and everything he owns into his teeny tiny space. Andy has three walls covered with cabinets, drawers, and compartments that house everything he needs, a bed that fits neatly within those cabinets, and a modest arrangement of furniture. While this might sound like his place is claustrophobic, it is surprisingly open and warm. Over the years through trial and error mixed with resourcefulness, Andy has figured out how to live well and richly in his small rent controlled apartment. He has surrounded himself with art and objects that reflect his life and tastes. He is constantly curating his possessions and getting rid of what he doesn't need. Andy loves his apartment and you feel it when you enter into it. He always says that if he didn't have this apartment he would never have survived the hustle and bustle of living in NYC for so many years. It is his place of safety and home within the chaos of life.

Whether it is a city, the country, or a suburb, we all need shelter and we all need a place to call home. Some people live in the same place their whole lives while others move frequently. Whether you live in a house, apartment, on a boat, or in a teepee, it is a natural instinct as humans to cultivate a nest. It doesn't need to be much, but we all feel the need to call something our own and to feel grounded.

In some cases, our environment is provided to us in a physical way that we have not chosen. If you live in a city, chances are you live in a smaller place with limited storage and space. If you live in the country, you may have more room but have to contend with the elements and animals. If you grew up abroad, you picked up ways of living from the culture you were surrounded by. Besides our homes, the other environment we spend a lot of time in is at work. The company you work for usually dictates how your cubicle is laid out or where your workstation is. These are all examples of products or situations dictated by external forces in our environment.

Oftentimes, we take habitats for granted and accept them the way they are. The thing is-*just because your living space or workspace was provided to you in one way, it doesn't mean it needs to stay that way.*

Like life, just because you find yourself in a particular situation, thought pattern, job, health, fitness, or relationship that isn't serving you, it doesn't mean that you can't change it at any point. The first thing is to recognize that there can be something to change. The second part is to know you have the strength and power to make the changes necessary to create the life you want and envision. The third part is to take the steps to make those changes. Like anything new, the hardest part is getting started, but once you're on a roll it gets easier and easier. *Clear* will help you with all these steps.

Exercise:

Throughout this book, you will engage in different writing exercises. Pick out a fresh journal or notebook that you love the look and physical feel of. Choose a pen that feels good in the hand and you like the color of--maybe this is the time you allow yourself to write with a sparkly purple pen. This notebook is going to be your base when working through *Clear*. Having one place where you write down your ideas and thoughts will allow you to go back at the end and see how far you have progressed. You might even want to personalize the journal by decorating it with positive images or sayings. It is your own personal journal, and you can do whatever you want with it. There is no right way to keep one.

Two
Unacceptable

We only accept our circumstances when we believe there is no other way.

Most of us get a feeling or intuition when things are not right in our lives. Whether or not we decide to act on these feelings is a whole other issue. Sometimes, we aren't even aware that the issues we are having are linked to other aspects of our lives. A lot of my clients come to me with various physical problems like stomach pain or body aches. I had a client, Lucie, who had an itch in her throat that she would describe as a chronic tickle. She felt it all the time and it became a constant distraction. Over the course of a year, she visited various doctors to find out what was causing the problem. As is typical in the Western world, we often look for diagnosis and pills to fix our problems without giving thought to the root of the cause. When we are diagnosed with an illness or condition, we can blame our issues on the condition rather than try to fix it by listening to what our bodies are trying to tell us. Lucie was always preoccupied by this tickle and none of the doctors she was going to could find a concrete origin. Each doctor would prescribe a new test or medicine to take. As we got Lucie's health into a better place by changing her diet and getting her on a regular exercise program, she started to see other areas of her life improve, such as her finances and work. However, the one area that she was continually unhappy with was in her personal relationships with her fiancé and family. The biggest issue she had with her fiancé was that they fought all the time and rarely conversed. Over the last three years, she had given up on talking to him. Although they lived together, they both avoided each other as much as possible. When asked why they stayed together, she said that it was because of the child they shared. The one thing they both agreed on was that they wanted to raise their child with two parents, but they couldn't take the steps to plan their wedding. During one of our sessions, I asked Lucie if she had ever thought that perhaps her throat was bothering her because she was not vocalizing her feelings to her fiancé or anyone in her life. She always held her feelings safeguarded inside, which gave off an aura that she was holding something back from people. It had taken a long time for me to gain her trust to open up to me about her personal life. The result of that session was transformative. Over the next few months, Lucie started to build courage and overcome her fear to tell people--her fiancé and family, in particular--what she thought and how she felt without shouting it through anger in the wrong words. Not only did the relationships in her life completely change and improve, within five months, the pain in her throat was gone.

Our bodies are smart. They know when something is not helping us to better ourselves. Usually, most of us experience this by getting an uncomfortable feeling in the pit of the stomach. That is our intuition is signaling us that something isn't right. Each of us is surrounded with a whirl of activity as our world becomes more connected, busy, and rushed. Our daily running around makes it hard to cut through all the noise to hear what our bodies are telling us and to see what is truly going on around us. It is easy to become disconnected from our thoughts and actions. Sometimes, a wake-up call may be in the form of getting sick or through the death of a loved one. Sometimes, it is literally by getting conked on the head from stuff falling off a shelf in a closet. In Lucie's case, her intuition quietly tapped her on the shoulder over a period of time. She initially decided to work with me because she had gained weight. Over the three years she'd had issues with her fiancé, she had started by experiencing sleepless nights which led to chronic tiredness, which led to weight gain, which led to being stressed all the time, which eventually led to the constant throat tickle and doctor visits. Had she not taken the steps to change, who knows where the malaise may have led. Whatever the case, if we ignore these intuitive feelings, they will continue to show up in our lives until we have no choice to pay attention. And in my experience, the sooner you recognize them and deal with them, the happier and more enjoyable life will become.

When we accept our circumstances as they are without questioning whether they can be better--function effortlessly, be more in line with our desires, or enhance the beauty in our lives--we keep ourselves from being successful. We prevent ourselves from living the best lives possible.

You will only grow as much as you allow yourself to. Believing you are only a product of your environment is a limiting belief and will prevent you from achieving greatness.

We all have the capability to change and develop throughout life. There is no age limit as to when this can happen. As a culture, we spend a lot of money on diets, books, therapists, clothes, cars, personal trainers, and plastic surgery in order to change and try to better ourselves. What people end up ignoring are their personal environments. How you physically live is a reflection of your mental wellbeing and vice versa. If you feel at all stagnant in your life or feel as though you aren't progressing in ways that you would like to, it may be time to look around at your environment.

Exercise:

What in your life do you just accept? While this can be hard to see in your own life, this exercise will help you to start opening your mind to thinking about it. Now is the time to take out your journal. At the top of a page write: What Am I Accepting? Write in a stream of consciousness fashion, letting the words onto the page without critiquing or self-correcting.

Here are some questions to get you started:

- What do you just accept in your relationships that you don't agree with? (How you spend your nights going out; how you communicate.)
- What do you accept at work? (What your position is at work; how much you make; what hours you work.)
- What do you accept in your daily activities? (No time to work out; eating dinner out instead of cooking at home.)
- What do you accept in the way you live? (Living in a rental versus buying a house; living in a cold climate instead of the warm one you like.)
- What do you accept about your life? (I can't go back to school now; vacations are too expensive.)

Three
Why We Live the Way We Do

No one is ever short on the excuses as to why they can't do something. Take, for instance, Frances--or Frankie as she was known as by her family--who had graduated high school and married young. By the time she was 25, she had three kids under the age of 6. Frankie loved her family and being a mother. She also worked part-time at a local mill to help support the family. Frankie had always wanted to go to college and to cultivate a career in business marketing. If she went to college, she would be the first from her family to go. Despite her desire, Frankie had her hands full with raising a family. She would say things like,

"When the kids are older I'll go back to school." When the kids got older, she said, "I can't afford this right now." Years later when her job offered tuition reimbursement and mentorship, she said, "I'm too old to start a new career." Although Frankie wanted to go back to college, she was too fearful to make the move to do it. All her excuses were real, but they weren't getting her to where she wanted to be in life.

What separates people who are successful from those who are not is awareness and action. People who believe in themselves and are willing to be fearless don't make excuses. They recognize what they are doing and move to change the action to serve them in a better way. When we accept a given situation or environment without question, we live from a place of fear. Change can seem like a scary thing because the outcome is not guaranteed. Our minds may lead us down a dark hole of negativity with "what-ifs," and "I don't know about this," and "I'm not good enough." From there, we convince ourselves of a myriad of excuses as to why we shouldn't or can't change. When you start to question why things are the way they are or whether something serves you, you begin to live from a place of empowerment. Through questioning, you can begin to see other possibilities you may never have imagined. This opens up the opportunity to make decisions that serve you and make your life better.

Living The Way Our Parents Did

But,… this is how my Mother used to do it.
(Or insert Father, Grandparent, etc)

I hate to break it to you, if you're reading this book, there is an 80-plus percent chance you don't live with your Mother anymore. If that is the case, why should she have a say in how you live today? This is an example of the excuses we use in our lives to not take responsibility for our own actions. When you were 10 years old, you *had* to listen to your Mother. She did know what was better for you and how to keep you safe. But, as soon as you become an adult, it's time to make your own decisions and become responsible for the outcomes of those decisions.

There is no denying that a lot of our habits and thought patterns are handed down from our parents. The idea of home is usually centered on our earliest memories from childhood. Those memories are tied to how our parents raised us, what kind of house they lived in, what kind of time they spent at home, and how they kept their house.

People link home to childhood upbringing and never question if this is how they currently want to live. The thought usually is, "If my parents did it this way and it worked for them, it must work for me."

Years ago I began to work with Amelie on making improvements to her diet. One day, I was showing her some healthy ways to cook in her kitchen when I noticed that she struggled to cut a butternut squash with a paring knife. I asked her where her other knives were. She responded rather briskly that her mother only ever used a paring knife and that she was a superb chef. "Fancy knives weren't necessary," she said.

I then asked her if she knew why her mother only used a paring knife.

In a later session, Amelie said, "You aren't going to believe this. I asked my mom why she only used a paring knife. She told me that when my siblings and I were young, money was tight and there was no extra money to buy a knife set. All she had was a couple of paring knives, which she became pretty adept at using. Once everyone was grown and she finally bought a full knife set, she wished she'd had it a lot sooner because it really changed her ability to cook."

Amelie was beside herself. She was upset that her Mother had gone through some challenging times and chose the wellbeing of her family over her own needs. She was also upset that she had suffered using a paring knife all those years because she had made assumptions about what the situation was, when in reality it was something completely different. She immediately went out and bought the best knife set she could afford.

⌘

It's important to keep in mind that what served your parents may not serve you. Times change. How people lived in the depression is certainly different than how people live today. While there may be many things that your parents do well, it is important to be judicious of which practices that you adopt into your life.

Believing that you need to emulate the way your parents lived will always keep you from being successful. It puts you in a place of living fearfully, with guilt, and afraid of change. These are all negative emotions that prevent progress. Without change, there can be no growth.

Exercise:

What do you find in your life that you do the same as the people who raised you? Do these habits help with how you want to live your life right now? Using the two prompts above, take 10 minutes to write down all the habits you have that are attributed to other people. One example might be holidays. Do you serve dinner like your mother did? Do you make certain dishes every year for Thanksgiving even though you or other people in your family don't like them? Perhaps you always go to a certain hardware store because that is the one your father always went to, despite knowing that you can get better prices online. Again, write your answers without a filter or judgment.

Matter of Money

If you believe that you'll never have the home of your dreams, you never will. We are only able to accomplish the things in life we believe we can. You may have many excuses as to why you will never own this home and the top reason will most likely be:

I will never make enough money to live in the house of my dreams.

Gayle had a habit of spending money she didn't have. Her favorite pastime was to shop-- either in stores or online. She used shopping as a way to relax, reward herself for working hard, and to feel better. Although Gayle wanted to own a house, she wasn't able to buy one because her credit was bad from her overspending. She was also in significant debt. Gayle needed to address her mindset around money and figure out other, healthier ways to deal with her life while aligning her finances. So we worked together to change those habits. Knowing it would take a few years to correct her finance issues and be in a position to buy a house, we collaborated to make Gayle's current apartment more relaxing and luxurious. Instead of seeking happiness through shopping, we instead focused on creating a home environment that would make her feel rewarded for her hard work. And we did it without spending much money. Gayle already owned a lot of things from her shopping sprees so we curated what she had. Anything she didn't need, she sold online and then used that money to round out a few things she needed to freshen up the place like paint and materials to fix some minor issues. In the end, by selling the things she didn't need and creating a home she didn't want to leave, she raised enough money to pay off some of her debt.

People incorrectly assume that it will take a lot of money to make the perfect home. First off, it isn't possible to have a perfect home, just like it is impossible to be an absolutely perfect person. Let's be honest, perfect is boring. The Japanese have a term called wabi-sabi which refers to perfection in the imperfect. There is no risk in perfection. If we don't take risks, there can be no change. Without change, there is no growth.

I have been inside plenty of amazing mansions over my career. But owning a lot of possessions or living in a gigantic house does not guarantee happiness. Likewise, you can be successful in life without living a fulfilling life. Our goal is to create surroundings that are positive reflection of our health and wellbeing.

It is possible to create a home that is beautiful and inspiring to *you* and its occupants.

You don't need a lot of money to make this happen. What you do need is an open mind and a willingness to dig deep to make changes.

Exercise:

What do you feel is holding you back from getting what you want in life financially? In your journal, take 10 minutes to write down everything you can think of where money feels like a block. When you are finished, look back through each item on the list and ask yourself, "Is it money or is it me?" Beside each item, mark it with either the word "money" or "me." How do the answers make you feel? How do you view your relationship with money? How can you take responsibility for making change in your life?

CLEAR

Four
What Our Environments Say About Us

Just like the clothes you choose to wear, your home and workplace say a lot about you and your mindset.

Roy had worked as an engineer at a local manufacturing plant for more than 25 years. He had a small windowless office that was tucked down in the basement level near the testing lab. Roy's was a Senior Product Engineer, but his ultimate goal was to break through to the Product Engineering Manager level. However, despite his tenure, he failed to make the transition and felt very frustrated by his position within the company.

Roy had been spent 8 years in his little office. The first think you notice when you walked into the space was how messy it was. Roy's desk was positioned close to the door, and there wasn't much room to stand inside the room. By default, most people stood uncomfortably in the doorway to talk to Roy. His desk was littered with papers, production parts, and tools. All the furniture in the room was old--most of which had been scavenged from different wings of the building that had undergone updates--and most of the drawers on the desk and cabinets didn't work properly. The windowless room was lit with old, yellowed fixtures that gave off a low pitch hum.

Roy had thoughtlessly accepted that this was his office given to him by his company. Although it had no natural daylight, the one thing he loved about the office was that it was separated from his colleagues, which provided him peace and quiet to get his work done. He did admit that the lack of daylight made him sleepy and a bit crabby some days. What Roy didn't realize was what his office presented the wrong message about him to his boss and coworkers. First, because of the location, Roy was out of sight and out of mind; It's hard to get promoted when people don't know you exist. Second, there was nowhere to sit down and have a conversation with him in his office. People felt awkward and uncomfortable with Roy when they stood in the doorway to talk to him. Would you want a manager that made people feel that way?

When people looked at the chaos on Roy's desk, it gave off the perception that he was unorganized and lacked detail. Again, would these be traits that you would want from a leader? Lastly, all the old furniture in his office showed that he felt like he didn't deserve the new pieces that had allocated throughout the building. As a manager, wouldn't Roy try to get the best resources he could to serve his team? Although he wanted the title and pay raise of a management position, he had never given thought to what it would take to *be* a manager. He just assumed that he deserved it because he'd put paid his dues for 25 years. He had never reflected on *why* he had not earned the promotion he desired. Instead, he blamed it on company politics, and with frustration, accepted it as is.

It wasn't until a yearly review with a new boss that Roy became aware of how he was perceived by his colleagues. Flabbergasted and scared about his future with the company, he lurched into action. He immediately hired me to help make changes in his life--we initially focused mindset and later we turned to his habitat. He first was asked that his office he relocated near his engineering colleagues. Within 3 months, he had a new desk with working drawers in a brightly lit cubicle. Surprisingly, he found he liked collaborating with his coworkers.

The move also gave him an opportunity to get rid of all the old stuff that had accumulated in his office over the years. He felt lighter and more invigorated in his new space. His colleagues noticed the change in him and remarked that he seemed like a new person. Overall, he felt happier and empowered to ask for what he needed to get his work done. He no longer feared being stuck in his position. For the first time in years, he felt like he had opportunity.

Like Roy, your environment speaks volumes about how you live your life, and what you believe about yourself and the people around you. You may say- I picked out this outfit, but I have to live in this apartment because it is the only one I can afford and it's a close drive to the office. Or, like Roy, who believed that his windowless, basement office at work was assigned to him and there is nothing he can do about it. Accepting your circumstances as they are will leave you in a position of living from fear and feeling overwhelmed.

Everything in your life is a manifestation of your thoughts. This includes your health, happiness, what your job is, where you live, how you live, if you are overweight, and your success in life. Changing your thinking is challenging and takes practice. We have thousands of thoughts per day. If you believe every thought that crosses your mind, you'll be in big trouble. It is important to be aware of your negative thoughts and limiting beliefs. When one comes across your mind, pause, accept it without judgment and move on. An example of a negative thought might, "I'm so fat." Instead of going down the path of negativity and following it up with, "These jeans make me look like a heifer;" "I can't believe I have all these rolls;" "Why can't I eat better?;" "I'm such a loser;" change the script. Those thoughts will never put you in place of empowerment or improved health. They will only make you feel worse. The better option is to *recognize* what you have said to yourself and then stop the vicious self-hate cycle. Try this instead: "I'm so fat. Ok. (Pause) Time to move forward." This is the first step to change your mindset and lead a more successful life. Remember, *you* have the ability to choose *where* you want live and *how* you want to live.

Personal Style

City, country, suburbs: raised ranch, McMansion, Tudor: modern, classic, contemporary…

There are a lot of ways to live and a lot of home options to choose from. No one style is correct or better than another. It all depends on the individual. Like the car you drive, it is a choice of what you like and how you want to be reflected.

Sometimes we inherit our style or taste from our family or culture. This isn't bad thing. It is different than just accepting a situation because you feel like you have no other choice. Deliberately deciding how you want to live gives you control over how you design the life you want.

Where we can run into problems is when we believe we need to choose a specific way of living to keep up appearances or because we feel the need to fit in. This leads to living a life of insecurity and fakeness, with continual feelings of not being good enough. *There is no authenticity or true joy in living someone else's life.*

Angela grew up by the New Jersey shore in an affluent town. Now 38, she had spent the majority of her life obsessed with her physical appearance. She also desperately wanted to fit in and possess all the nice things her friends had. Angela She worked really hard at her job as a nurse, but she never felt like she was getting ahead. So, she worked overtime to be able to afford name-brand clothes; hair straightening appointments; perfect nails; and tanning and gym memberships at top-of-the-line clubs. She leased an expensive luxury car and lived in a large Mediterranean-style house with her husband and dogs in a gated community by the ocean. On the outside, it looked like Angela had "made it." However, her lifestyle cost a lot of money to maintain and the stress this placed on her life began to take a toll. Over the years she developed a host of physical issues--from disordered eating to try to stay skinny to anxiety.

A wakeup call came at 38 when she was diagnosed with breast cancer. Her fight cancer made Angela question how she had lived her life and what was important to her. She realized that all the choices she had made were based on what her friends had and not on any true desire of her own. After significant thought, Angela was finally able to admit that she was incredibly unhappy with her life and felt overwhelmed. She viewed the cancer as an opportunity to start over. As she went through treatment, she began to outline what was truly important to her and how she wanted to live. She knew that she loved being a nurse and helping people, but realized that her abilities were stunted by the unnecessary stress she had created in her life. She decided to relocate with her husband to South Carolina where she could still be by the ocean, but instead live in an area that was more casual, slower paced, and less expensive. They settled in a country style home that reflected her new laidback lifestyle, and downsized to make the home cozier and easier to maintain. No longer faced with significant financial burden, Angela spent less time working and more time with her husband. In addition, she began to pursue new interests like kayaking and jewelry making. She let her logoed clothes go and over the next few years replaced them with outdoor gear that fit her new lifestyle. She has been cancer-free for five years.

One of the main takeaways Angela learned was to be more deliberate in how she chose to live. Through self-analysis, she learned to cultivate *her* personal style, not a fabricated style she had used to keep up appearances.

Our lives are a marathon, not a sprint. We grow and change over time. So can your personal environments. Seek help when you need to by reaching out to interior designers, reading design magazines or watching home improvement TV channels. Sometimes, we need help when we are a little stuck.

The best thing you can do when it comes to style is practice listening to your inner voice. You know deep down whether you like or hate something and whether it will serve you or not. You don't need anyone to tell you that. Use your home as a place to experiment and gain confidence with your decisions. That is fearless living.

Exercise:

Do you have a style? How would you define it? Here is a chance to get creative. In your journal, describe your style. Use words or if you feel like it, cut out photos from magazines that show what your style is like and paste them into your journal. If you don't feel like you have a particular style, what kinds of styles do you like? Describe those styles or use images to illustrate what they are. Take a look through fashion, design, or special interest magazines and use images that you find appealing. As you pick out images you like andput them together, you will begin to see certain themes come together. Collectively, these can be defined as a style. Have fun with this exercise. Don't worry if the images don't reflect how you currently live your life. Your journal is a safe place to explore new ideas and ways of living.

Our Stuff

Everything in your possession is a choice. Both a burden and a blessing, our stuff can weigh us down or set us free. The same can be said about our thoughts.

Reis loved motorcycles and everything about the moto culture. He enjoyed riding motorcycles, owning them, working on them, and his community of motorcycle friends. What Reis loved most about motorcycles was they gave him the freedom to get on a bike and ride wherever he wanted. When he rode, he felt completely focused and in the flow with his machine. They were his escape his everyday worries and allowed him time to relax and be alone. He always returned from a ride energized and full of fresh ideas for work and his life.

Over the years, Reis accumulated a variety of bikes. At first, he bought them because he wanted to have different styles to ride, from vintage to dirt bikes. However, his interest soon became more of an obsession. He went from having five bikes to 55, or so he thought. He wasn't entirely sure how many he had because they were stored at different locations since he had outgrown his garage. He had some at friend's houses, his own garage, and other spaces he was renting out.

Reis began to feel burdened by owning all these bikes. More than half of them didn't run. Much to the chagrin of his family, he spent most of his nights working on the bikes to either maintain them or make them operable. The cost of maintaining the bikes was more than his family could afford. He also spent less time riding with the community that had gotten him into bikes in the first place. The motorcycles had taken over his life. What had initially started as a positive way to relax and free Reis from the stresses of everyday life had become a burden to him and his loved ones. Reis decided to sell the majority of his bikes when he overheard his son tell a friend that he thought his Father loved his motorcycles more than his family. Heartbroken, Reis realized the impact he had on his son. With the money he raised from selling off his collection, he bought two new, maintenance free, motorcycles- one for himself and one for his son.

What we decide to own is a reflection of our interests, taste, status, knowledge, personality, and history. It is a reflection of how we live, love, and what we believe. As such, it is imperative to be discerning about what you possess or you run the risk of those things possessing you. Everything you own is a product of your environment and holds energy. What you give off, your possessions absorb. Any insecurity, body-hate, or relationship issue that you are dealing with is associated with your stuff.

The reality is we use very few of our overall possessions. If we do not consistently go through our stuff, clutter accumulates. Like negative thoughts, clutter crowds us from living freely and to our greatest potential. When I work with clients on their environments, the first thing we deal with is clutter. Everyone has some. It is the most important aspect to change and the one that is met with the most resistance. When you accumulate a lot around you, it is because there is some aspect of your life that is lacking and it is usually rooted in fear.

This is a very hard thing for people to accept. People are resistant to let go of their possessions because a lot of intense feelings, memories, and situations can arise. It feels easier to live with the out-of-sight-out-of-mind mentality. Junk? What junk? Although, like that feeling inside that tells you something isn't right, clutter always causes anxiety, which is a clue that something isn't right. Clutter is the number one reason people fight in any given space.

While people may resist the process, they always feel completely liberated afterwards. By getting rid of the junk, they find their lives to change in ways they could have never have imagined. It is important to never force someone into getting rid of his or her possessions, unless they are a hoarder and in potential harm. Change needs to come from within.

Owning less and carefully curating your environment with needed possessions enhances your life and is incredibly freeing. It allows beauty to shine in and gives you the space to be fearless.

Exercise:

How much do you own? Do you consider what you own to be a necessity or superfluous? Time to take that journal out again. Write a list of the major possessions you own. Car? House? Clothes? Collections? What is most important to you? Take time to reflect and take stock of what things you store and use daily.

Five
Accepting The Way We Live

The two biggest areas that we occupy in our lives are our homes and workspace. These habitats are where we have personal belongings and spend a lot of time. Your environments are energetically a reflection of what is going on in your life. If there is any area in your life that needs work, it will show up in your environment.

Tess was obsessed with food. She always talked about what she could or could not eat. She continually tried new diets and approaches to weight loss, but she could never seem to lose the 10 pounds she so desperately wanted to drop. Despite lifting weights and training for half marathons, she saw a change in her physique. This had been going on for more than 5 years.

When you looked into Tess' refrigerator, it was a mess. The shelves and drawers were dirty and packed with expired produce, bits of leftover food wrapped in half open plastic wrap, and jumbles of packaging from condiments. In addition, the refrigerator was shoved into a tight spot which made it difficult to open the doors.

While she didn't realize it, Tess' refrigerator was a reflection of her relationship and struggle with food. It was a giant "elephant" that was shoved into the corner of the room, horribly neglected. Tess' goal was to lose weight, but she didn't focus on how to nourish her body and mind.

She also failed to nourish many other areas of her life. For example, she set external goals at work and financially, but did not consider how attaining those goals would affect her personally. She didn't even know why she wanted to achieve those goals, aside from thinking that it was the right thing to do.

To look in the fridge was to look inside Tess' mind. She was disorganized (food on top of food), uncommitted yet not willing to give up on dead-end goals and behaviors (keeping leftover food scraps until they rotted), and felt like a mess.

Frustrated with the lack of progress she experienced in almost every facet of her life, Tess decided to make some changes. In order to make a change with her relationship to food, she needed to first respect the food she put into her body and so she moved the fridge to more accessible location. She then cleaned and organized the fridge so that she could make room to receive the nourishment from the food and consciously honor the process of eating well. When her fridge was set up and looking pretty, she discovered that she enjoyed cooking. It was no longer a struggle to get food in and out of the fridge or to remember what was in it. She became more consciously aware of what she put in her mouth and how it nourished her body. Eventually, she focused less on dieting and began to embrace a truly healthy lifestyle. Unsurprisingly, she dropped the 10 pounds.

When Tess became aware of her negative thoughts and limiting beliefs, she became able to take the steps to change the habits that prevented her from seeing success. Similarly, the first step she took toward healing her home and aligning it to be a reflection of her greatest self helped her become more aware of her environment and the affect it has on her.

We go through so much of our days half

aware. We are distracted by our phones- texting, surfing the web, answering calls. We have families we take care of and who demand our attention. At work we have endless emails and meetings. How many times have you driven somewhere and cannot remember how you got there or sat through a movie and can't recall what it was about?

We do the same thing, daily, with our living spaces. We rush through our rooms in the morning to get ready for work without noticing the floor under our feet. Is it cool? Has the sun, coming through the window, warmed up a spot? At night, we come home and barely put together a decent meal, flop on the couch and zone out in front of the TV without talking much to the other people in the house.

Can you describe where you live? I don't mean in the "I-live-in-a-yellow-house on Oak Lane-kind of way. I mean, can you describe it in detail like this? –

When I walk across the uneven slate walkway to my front door painted orange with translucent glass, there is a welcoming group of volunteer morning glories that grow around one of the white painted posts on the front porch.

We become so disconnected from where we live, we don't notice any details. Have you ever sat in one place in a room and really looked at it? Have you taken in where all the objects and furniture are? Where the light comes in and at what time of day? The noise coming from outside or made from within the room? Have you seen where the dust or the stray crumbs settle on the floor or how the pet fur collects in the weave of the fabric on the sofa? Do you see where you let clutter accumulate? Are you able to move freely around the room or do you have to step over papers and toys? How does the room feel to you? Is it cold, drafty, hot, or stuffy? Do you like being in the room or do you always avoid it? Just like becoming aware of your thoughts, it is important to become aware of your surroundings.

Exercise:

Using your journal and keeping the above questions in mind, pick a room in your home that you don't particularly like or spend very little time in. Find a spot in that room to sit. If there is no seating available, sit on the floor as comfortably as you can.

Take a minute to focus on your breathing. Breathe in through your nose and out through your mouth. Quiet your mind down and allow yourself to become present in the room. Begin to become aware of your surroundings. Without judgment, take in the details. In your journal, record your observations. When you are done with the room, continue to work through your home, yard, and workspace. Make sure to include attics, basements, storage sheds, and garages.

This exercise can cause a lot of anxiety in people. They start to become aware of the chaos around them, which they have been ignoring, and immediately go into panic mode and feelings of no good. How can I be living this way? My (Parent, Spouse, etc) would be so disappointed in me. I can't even keep a clean house! I'm such a failure at life. I have no one to help me fix the leaky faucet. I can't stand the pet fur everywhere. The garbage needs to be taken out. I can't get to that project until I move all this crap out of the way. I hate that (Spouse, Children, Roommate) never does his dishes. I'm the only one who ever does the laundry!

The point of the exercise isn't to make you feel bad or to fix anything. It is solely to become aware of your surroundings and start the process of figuring out what works and doesn't work for you without judgment. How you are living right now is exactly how you should be living. Being aware that change is possible will allow you to develop a plan to create a beautiful environment that you feel love and inspiration in.

Working/Living Around Issues

I lived in an apartment for years where there was a bathroom that had a medicine cabinet hung high. It was little, probably only eleven by eighteen inches and must have been put up by a tall guy. I'm pretty short and could only see from my chin up in it. The toilet and bathtub weren't situated where I could stand on them to see more of my body in this little mirror. I was stuck with this little itty-bitty area and only my face to look at. From the chin down, there are a whole lot of parts that can have issues before you're ready to step out for your day. Such as, is your shirt buttoned up all the way? Did you drop toothpaste down your front? I have long hair and could only see part of it in the mirror. At a job I had during that time, my coworkers used to tease me about my crazy hair. No joke, it looked fine from the top and front, but there was a party going on in the back that I was completely oblivious to!

I would walk everyday into the bathroom, look in the mirror and get pissed. I hate this mirror! Who would hang it this high? What an idiot! I need to change this! Then, I would walk out and completely forget about it. Do you know how many times you walk in and out of a bathroom on a given day? A lot! I would say, at the very least, three times a day. Here is the crazy part; I lived with this situation for over eight years!!! That is an average of going into the bathroom 8,760 times over that period and feeling unhappy.

Although this mirror wasn't serving me, I worked around it. I didn't want to do the work to change it. Besides forgetting about it when I left the room, I made up a lot of excuses for why it wasn't worth changing. - This is just a rental. I don't want to invest any money into it when I'm just going to leave. I don't have the time to look for a replacement. I don't want to spend the time working on this when I'm already working so many hours. Who will help me with this? It will take two people to hang and no one will want to help me. If I take the old one down, I should probably paint the room as well. It's looking dingy, but I don't want to get into a big project. On and on it went.

I can assure you that during the same time, I was doing the same thing in many aspects of my life. While I thought I could work around this issue, it kept rearing its head daily; remember about three times a day. I just wasn't acknowledging it. The same thing was happening with my health, my job, and my relationships. I was working around issues that were not serving me and were holding me back from being truly successful.

I reached a point where enough was enough. I was really unhappy with my life and tired of being a victim. When I decided that I needed change and started to pursue it in my life in order to live a life that I designed versus one that was just given to me, a lot of things began to move.

Fear keeps us from making changes. Although I had always considered myself confident, I didn't know that I was making a lot of choices in my life based on fear. I can't change this mirror because I'm afraid I won't have the money to buy the one I want. I won't be able to hang the new mirror because I am afraid there will be no one to help me do it. I don't want to do the work because I am afraid it will take time away from other more worthwhile pursuits. These thoughts were ridiculous, but they were a part of my everyday thinking. The fear-based thoughts were keeping me from making a change and doing something that would make me happy. I couldn't even admit that I was having fear thoughts because that felt like a weakness to me and I was hell bent on being a strong woman. I didn't realize that strength comes from vulnerability.

As I began to make changes in my health, fitness, and mindset, I decided to finally address the mirror issue. My environment had been sending me signals and I was done ignoring them. That bathroom was a reflection, literally, of my old self and thought patterns. I was ready to change the image in the mirror and fix the problem so I could live more fearlessly. Once I made the decision to do so, a funny thing began to happen.

All the fears I had made up in my mind as to why I couldn't do it, vanished.

I ran into my landlord, who I had a good relationship with, and asked if she was ok with me switching out my mirror while I explained why. She said, of course, and said to take the purchase of it off rent. Score! Paid for and it is so much easier to shop for things when you have a budget. It narrows your options to make a decision. After eight years, the room was looking a bit dingy. Forced air heat had left a residue on the walls and the people who had built the room had been sloppy in their painting. Although I knew that I was going to move in the future, I couldn't control when that would exactly happen. I decided to paint the room because I knew having a fresh color would make me happy immediately. It would put me living in the present, which I had control over, versus living in a future, which I did not yet have control over. When I decided to paint, I decided to also attack a few other things that were bothering me. I could use more storage, so I hung shelves and I wanted a better place to hang my towels so I moved the towel bar. Since I was moving everything around the bathroom to make room to work, I went through all my clutter and got rid of anything that had an expired date or that I hadn't used in a while. It felt so good to throw all these old used up things away. It also gave me a lot more room in my new medicine cabinet. That fear that no one would help me hang the new medicine cabinet? Oh yeah, the only thing I needed to do was ask for help. My partner not only immediately helped, he did it for me. How long did it take to do the whole project? A total of six hours over the course of one week working a couple hours here and there after my daily work was done. Considering how many years I had wasted being upset, this was a small investment of time. While I had initially dreaded the entire project, I ended up enjoying the whole process because I was so excited to see the results.

When I was done, I was so happy and proud! I went from hating my bathroom to loving it. I had created a beautiful and calm surrounding. I started to take better care of myself by treating my body with love and attention. I started using a body brush and taking long baths with Epsom salt, regularly. My stuff was better organized with the new shelves, and I had gotten rid of many things that were no longer serving me. The overall bathroom functioned better with the changes and made my life easier. The best part was the LARGE mirror hung at the proper height. I could now see myself from my thighs to beyond the top of my head. I could truly start to see what I looked like and tame the crazy hair. Sometimes, we aren't aware of how we appear outwardly when we spend so much time inside our minds, just like we aren't aware that our environment is a reflection of what is going on in our lives.

The old mirror and bathroom was illustrating that I was settling for the way I perceived my life to be. I believed the little image in the mirror and that I was a small part of my world. I believed that things just happened to me and that I was a victim in the circumstances. I did not feel empowered or capable to make changes. Making the decision to work on the bathroom was supporting the changes that I was making in my life to become a more successful person. It gave me the opportunity to take a good look in the mirror and decide how I wanted to be viewed in the world and how I wanted to live my life. Getting rid of the old medicine cabinet and issues helped me to let go of unnecessary fears and embrace beauty into my environment.

What Are You Working Around?

When we begin to wake up to the environment around us, we begin to become aware of the issues around us that are not serving to make our lives better. As with my bathroom situation, everyone has a version of this in his or her lives. Perhaps, you do some of the following things. -

> Do you have a habit of dropping all your stuff right by the front door as you enter your house causing you to step over it every time you walk by?

> Is your desk covered in stack of papers you have never looked at, but keep because you think you will?

> Do you always have a pile of dishes in the sink and can never cook something before you root through it to find your pan?

These are some examples of things that we work around without giving any thought to how they impact our lives. These seemingly small things add up and create an environment of chaos, frustration, and defeat. How can you grow and excel in an environment like that? Most likely, you find a lot of ways to avoid these areas of your house. They are physically ugly. When you look at them you get an anxious feeling deep down that is trying to signal to you that something isn't right.

You probably even say to yourself- that pile of papers on my desk is stressing me out! But, you don't do anything about it. Instead you go into the kitchen and start eating out of the peanut butter jar because you think that will make you feel better. We both know, it never does. That is fear-based living. By avoiding those situations in your environment, you are avoiding other aspects in your life. When we avoid things, we do not have the opportunity to change them.

With the previous exercise, you have started to become aware of how you live and are accepting it without judgment. The next step is to be honest with yourself and identify what issues you are working/living around.

Exercise:

Take out your journal and open to a fresh page. Make a list of ten areas of your habitat or issues you are working/living around. Don't over think it. Just write what first comes to your mind. Your list may be shorter than ten items. It can be pages long. Don't worry. Just get it all out of you. When you are done writing, read through the list. Identify the top three that make you the most anxious and unhappy. Those will be the areas you are going to start working with.

In the next Part, I will walk you through how to make changes to clear the areas in your life that are bogging you down and keeping you from being successful.

It is time to start living fearlessly.

ANNICK MAGAC

Part Two

Clutter

Six

Clutter Effect

This entire section is dedicated to clutter because it is the most important--and inhibiting--aspect of any area that you occupy. I'm talking about all that stuff that collects in and around your home and office. Whether it belongs to you, your family or roommates, clutter can be classified as anything you do not use or love. It involves having too many possessions in too small of an area, which creates a disorganized and chaotic space. It can also include anything that is unfinished in your life like that book you just can't seem to finish or a painting you gave up on. Dealing with the clutter will simplify your life, allow beauty into your surroundings and give you the emotional room to live fearlessly, ultimately leading to more success.

Years ago, I met with a woman named Isabel who experienced significant struggle. She had spent $100,000+ on a kitchen renovation in hopes of designing the most beautiful space with top of the line appliances and gorgeous finishes. She'd hoped these renovations would enhance the cooking experience and make her an exceptional chef. Also overweight, she believed that she would be inspired to prepare nutritious meals that would help her whittle her waist. Isabel also silently believed this kitchen would become a showcase for how successful and perfect her life was. The dirty secret? There was crap in her cabinets, on the counter and floor, and the sink was always filled with dirty dishes. The clutter in Isabel's kitchen robbed the beauty from the room. Despite all the hard work and money she had put into beautifying the space, Isabel found that she never wanted to be in the kitchen, and nor did anyone else.

Isabel quickly lost interest in cooking and grew frustrated that, despite the new kitchen, she remained unable to lose weight. Instead of eating home-cooked meals at her gorgeous dining room table, she and her family gobbled fast food in front of the television.

Isabel explained to me that a few years later she began to lament about how she used to love to cook and always thought that she should get back into it. At that point, she lost the many years she could have spent practicing to become a better chef. She also missed out on spending precious time with the loved ones she now rarely sees. She felt badly about herself and wished for things to be different.

It didn't need to be like this, I explained to Isabel. She can have the stellar gourmet kitchen, learn to be an incredible chef, have family and friends around her that she loves, and feel pretty damn good about herself.

Has clutter negatively impacted your life as it did Isabel's? Continue reading to see how clutter can affect your life and what you can do to turn its challenges into triumphs.

જ⊙ન

Vivian had a studio she worked out of for her interior design practice. She had previously worked out of her house for 2 years before she was able to bring her business to the next level and acquire a more professional space with an office where she could meet clients. The studio signified a transition in Vivian's career as a businesswoman and designer.

When she first moved into the new space, she was excited, proud, and inspired to see the growth of her business. Using her design talents, she created a beautiful vibrant space that showcased her talents and felt welcoming to her clients. She experienced such significant growth over the next couple of years that she brought on two assistants to help with the influx of projects. Vivian felt like she was headed in the right direction.

Three years later, things had changed drastically. Vivian was a mother, her marriage was on the rocks, and her business suffered. One of her assistants had quit, which was somewhat good because she no longer had enough projects to sustain the employee. She felt drained and uninspired. The only bright element of her life was motherhood--which she loved--but Vivian felt all the other aspects of her life were in limbo.

When you entered her studio there was a sense of tension and chaos. There were piles of fabric swatches, tile samples, and paint chips littered all over. The studio was so overstuffed that there wasn't a free chair for a client to sit on. Vivian and her employee bickered constantly. The décor of the space looked worn and out of style. She had stopped receiving her clients to the studio, as she was ashamed for them to see it. Vivian felt suffocated and creatively stunted in the space. Worse still, she and her employee had begun to bicker regularly. She knew she needed to her life, both personally and professionally.

Vivian decided to start her transformation where she felt most comfortable and gave the studio an overhaul. She asked her assistant to go through their inventory of samples and remove anything they had not used on a project. Together, they did a deep clean and came up with a plan to rearrange and update the décor of the studio.

While working closely with her assistant on this project, Vivian realized that she could trust him and decided to promote him. She put him in charge of the design and build of projects. She continued to interface with clients, but was now able to free up her schedule to spend more time with her family. Vivian felt more energetic and was newly inspired to take on her challenges in life. She also felt a flood of fresh creative ideas to implement into her business.

Everything in the world is connected and contains energy. Our bodies have energy. Nature has energy. The food we eat has energy. Our possessions and the buildings we occupy have energy. In order for energy to be positive, it needs to have movement and clarity. When energy gets stagnant, it becomes clutter. Linked to the law of attraction, clutter attracts more clutter, which increases stagnation and negativity.

When our lives are balanced and we have good health, love, and faith, we tend to create lots positive space around us. Our skin and eyes are clearer. We attract great people and experiences into our lives. Our environments reflect our balance and become more beautiful. Conversely, when our lives are unbalanced and unhealthy, and we feel lonely and fearful, the space around us constricts. Our skin and eyes look dull. We attract negative and hurtful experiences into our lives to affirm how horrible everything is. Our environments reflect our imbalances and begin the emotional and physical clutter we surround ourselves with makes us feel suffocated and overwhelmed.

Clutter can also physically affect your health; it collects dust and stale air in your home. It can attract vermin and filth, which creates a hazardous health environment. The stagnant energy can make you feel tired and unmotivated. It can even affect your body weight. Have you noticed that most hoarders tend to be overweight?

Clutter can affect your relationships and can be the root cause of many arguments. It is one of the larger issues of contention in marriages and cohabitation. It can create a physical and emotional barrier between you and other people. It can affect the way people treat you and make you feel ashamed.

It can affect you financially as you spend money on things that you do not need or cannot afford. Clutter can cause you to procrastinate and to be disorganized. One of the biggest burdens of clutter is that it can keep you living in the past and in a victim mindset. Remember, our surroundings are a reflection of our inner self.

Exercise:

What areas of your life do you feel are stagnant? Take out your journal and open to a new page. Take 5 to 10 minutes to respond to the following questions:

- Identify three areas of your life you feel stuck. Is it in a relationship? Career? Health and fitness? Finances? Etc.?

- Why do you feel you are stuck? Do not overthink your response. Allow yourself to write in a non-critical stream of consciousness fashion.

Seven
Overwhelmed To Empowered

"I'm so stressed out." I hear this a lot each day from clients, friends and family. Riley, a close friend, said this phrase every time we spoke. As a mother of three, she juggled schedules; worked a high profile job as a vice president of a marketing firm; and felt pressured to look young and fit while heading toward the big "5-0" birthday. At 49, Riley was overweight, scattered, forgetful, tired, and constantly anxious which made her snippy both to her family and coworkers. She felt stagnant at work, her home was a mess, and her new car kept breaking down. She dreaded her upcoming birthday because she felt her life should be

different than it was. However, she wasn't willing to change anything she was currently doing.

When a client comes to me, it's usually because they seek to change their lives and become more successful with their goals. The first area most people want to improve is their health and fitness. More specifically, they yearn to lose weight and get into shape. I can set a client up with a program that will guarantee them to lose weight. However, in order for them to have sustained success and keep the weight off, their mindset needs to be addressed. If it isn't, they will bounce back up to their original weight. Oftentimes they gain more weight than they lost, which makes them feel more miserable because they now have a concrete reason to feel like a failure. Everything in our lives is connected. If a person feels like they lack in any one area--relationships, spirituality, family, or money--this will affect their mindset, bodies, and any other part of their lives.

We crave change. Our society is obsessed by it. We love to see "before-and-afters" related to body transformations and home renovations. We love a good story about the under dog coming from behind to win against all odds. Despite our obsession with transformation, we have a hard time embracing change ourselves. We are okay watching from afar, but have a hard time taking the steps to start the process in our own lives. However, true success occurs when we are fearless and continue to change throughout our lives despite what obstacles we may face.

People want to change and can recognize that change will be beneficial for them. Our bodies are smart. We know everything we *should* do--eat more veggies and exercise regularly, for example. Whether or not we do it is a whole other thing. Fear raises its ugly head at the scent of change and can quickly cause a person to feel overwhelmed and eventually, paralyzed.

I often see this with clients who are in relationships they have outgrown.

Colin had dated and lived with his girlfriend from college for the past 8 years. Throughout the 2 years we had worked together, he complained about how much he wanted to end the relationship and date other people. When I asked why he stayed in it, he would say he couldn't afford NYC rent alone and he needed to save up money to move. *This went on for more than 2 years.* Colin knew what he wanted, but his fear of change led to excuse after excuse as to why he couldn't end the relationship.

His relationship woes also manifested physically in his apartment. The bedroom he shared with his girlfriend was tiny, which is typical in New York City. The bed took up the majority of the room and there was stuff everywhere. Clutter was piled on the floor, all over the dressers, and the bed was never made. Colin admitted that he hated spending time in that room and often slept on the couch at night.

I immediately suggested that he and his girlfriend work on the clutter in the bedroom.

They picked a Sunday to go through everything they'd stuffed into that tiny room. Working together, they talked more than they had in the past 6 months. As they de-cluttered the room, it became clear that neither of them was fulfilled in the relationship. They came to the conclusion that they did not fit in the room together--*physically or* mentally. By the end of the night, they came to the mutual decision to separate.

Clutter is a manifestation of energy that is stuck. When we get rid of clutter, it changes everything and takes us from feelings of overwhelm to a position of empowerment. We can see the physical release of objects. Although, initially fearful, it is incredibly satisfying to get rid of stuff. You have the power to decide what is important to you and serves you well and what does not. You have control over creating the habitat that you want to live or work in. It does not control you unless you allow it to. Removing clutter allows energy in our environment to flow and releases us from the burden of our past. It takes away excuses that have been used to hold us back from change and opens pathways for new energy to flow in. It makes room for new possibilities and opportunities to enter into our lives. It gives us a fresh vitality to conquer things we want to do.

The less you have around you the more you are able to stand out and lead your own life. This allows you to break free from your self-made baggage and to transition to a place of empowerment. That is how you live fearlessly.

Exercise:

Do you feel overwhelmed? Take your journal and find a quiet peaceful place to write. Does that even sound overwhelming to you? Don't overthink it. A quiet place might be a favorite chair in your home, a warm bath, or a local café. The point is to slow down for 10 minutes and take a break. Before you open your journal, take three deep breaths in through your nose and out through your mouth. The three breaths will help calm your mind from racing at warp speed about the bazillion things you need to accomplish today. Now open your journal. Make a list of the things in your life you currently find overwhelming. Once you are done, review the list. What items could you get help with? What items could you let go? What items can you go from feeling overwhelmed to empowered by changing the way you think or react to them?

Eight

What Hoarders Teach

Several years ago I was asked by a loved one to help a family clear out a hoarder's home. I agreed because of my love for the family, and to be honest, I had no idea what I was getting involved in. It ended up being an incredibly insightful and horrific experience at the same time.

The grandmother of the family, Grams, who was in terrible health, was the hoarder and owned the house. Grams was confined to a wheelchair and lived on the first floor of her home with no access to a proper bathroom or functioning kitchen. There was so much stuff in the house that you could barely open the front door to walk in. There was a narrow path to where she lived, which was about a five-by-five-foot area within the living room. From there, narrow paths meandered throughout the house. None of which were big enough to get a wheelchair through.

Grams had inherited the home from her parents who had also been hoarders. The house had already held her parents' belongings. They were heavily involved with the community and church, and when people passed away within their community, Grams' parents helped settle estates. Whatever was not inherited was collected into the home. Also, over the years, there were always waves of various people living in the house who also left stuff behind. Grams now had ownership of the possessions of countless people, including her own and that of her deceased husband.

As is common with hoarders, Grams lived a secluded existence. She had estranged relationships with her family. Everyone around her wanted to help both with her health and with her home. However, she refused the help and acted like a martyr with a victim mindset. When she declined the help, she'd say things like, "You could never help me in the way I need," or, "I keep all of this for you." At the same time, she was ashamed to have people in her house and since she couldn't leave, she saw people less and less. Within the same time period, her beloved dog also passed away from old age.

People from her church and community continued to offer her help with her home, but he would not let anyone touch her stuff. She had used all the clutter around her to create a physical and mental fortress that no one could enter.

One day, a family member found Grams passed out on the floor. No one was certain how long she'd been there. When the ambulance came, as can be imagined, they had a difficulty getting to her and pulling her from the house. Sadly, Grams ended up in the hospital for a long length of time. However, her family decided it was the perfect opportunity for an intervention.

I had been in and out of the house a few times over the years, but I was unprepared for the disarray it had dissolved into. The first thing that hit you as you entered the front door was the putrid smell. We immediately donned facemasks, pants, long sleeve shirts, and gloves. I covered my head, as well. There was no way I would expose my body to this toxic environment. The second thing to hit me was a wave of emotion. The house felt constricted, burdened, sad, and angry--this was in addition to all the feelings that came up for the people helping, which was mainly family.

Where to begin? It felt incredibly overwhelming. We all just stood in the small clearing looking around trying to decipher to where the dining room should be. Yes, *should be*. There was nothing in that mess to indicate that there was a dining room with a table, china cabinet, and chairs. All you could see was a mountain of plastic bags, papers, and unidentifiable stuff.

So many questions faced us. What to keep? What to throw away? Was there anything of value? Was there money hidden anywhere? We started to gingerly go through things. All you could hear was, "Oh My God! Ewwwww! No way. Nooooo way! Look at this!"

We quickly realized that there was nothing of value in all of this clutter. There were no heirlooms of family ancestry, precious jewelry, or rare coins. There was, however, an inordinate amount of jars filled with miscellaneous buttons; bags sealed within bags with envelops filled with neatly folded used packaging from fast food restaurants; old bandages with dried blood on them; photos that no one could identify a single person in; old letters and postcards; newspaper clippings in envelops with names of unknown people written on them; old subway tokens; broken pieces of furniture; outdated electronics; worn clothes; knickknacks; cheap memorabilia from trips we weren't sure she had ever been o; loose change; and boxes with teeth in them. The teeth were truly a mystery. None of us could phantom why Grams had held onto any of it. Nor could we discern why she always insisted that great treasures were hidden within.

The filth was overpowering. Of all the vacuums that we uncovered--four in all--not a single one of them worked. It was no wonder that Grams had lived with open sores on her legs, which never healed. The environment was completely unsanitary. There was a lot of dry heaving throughout the day from various people as they would uncover bags of rotten bandages, used tissues and toilet paper. I had never witnessed anything like this in my life, nor had anyone else. It took a long time to get through everything.

By the end of the day, people had stopped looking through the bags and just started chucking them out a window into the bed of a truck. The overall feeling was, get me out of here and get this crap as far away from me as possible. After clearing the first floor of the modest-sized house, there were five full sized pick-up truck loads of overflowing garbage bags and three truck loads of scrap metal sent off for recycling.

The whole experience was incredibly emotionally draining. Being exposed to such a horrific environment was one thing. But seeing first hand how the actions of one person could affect a whole family and community was another. While Grams had initially collected and kept the clutter because of a myriad of personal issues, her unwillingness to allow help into her life caused pain and distress among all the people around her. I don't think that anyone becomes a hoarder with a vengeful intent, but this example serves to show that our actions affect others. Specifically, actions that we know deep down are not even good for ourselves.

After the house was cleared, cleaned, and tidied, everyone became really nervous about breaking the news to Grams, who was still in the hospital. Under most circumstances, a hoarder should be involved in the process of getting rid of their clutter. However, this particular circumstance posed a significant risk to her safety and health.

The family had no desire to pilfer any treasures they found. They only yearned to put aside all resentment and to have a relationship with their mother/grandmother in her final years.

Grams' daughter broke the news to her from a place of love and compassion. For all the fear everyone had, a miraculous thing occurred. Grams returned to her house and kept the place clutter-free. She started to receive visitors from her church and have better communication with her family. Her health improved significantly. Though, a few years later she had a stroke and into her daughter's home, which had always been the want of her family. Grams had always resisted moving because she was scared to leave her home. By moving into her daughter's house, she was surrounded by love, vibrant life, and the help she needed. Grams never asked or wanted for a single possession that had been thrown away.

❧❧

Although you may not be a hoarder, it is important to keep in mind how your current actions can affect the people around you and the generations behind. We can have the best intentions in mind, but we need to ensure that what we do is in line with what we want.

Exercise:

What are you hoarding? Open your journal and take into consideration the following questions and write your answers in the journal:

- Is there anything you are afraid of letting go of?

- Is there anything you keep multiples of, just in case?

- How would you feel if you let those possessions go?

Nine

You Are Not Your Possessions

People have a hard time getting rid of clutter because they feel they are also getting rid of a part of themselves or their past. They often hold on to things due to guilt and obligation. The biggest protest is, "But I may need it someday!

Liza, a mother of four, recognized that she needed help in the environment part of her life. When I initially work with clients, I have them rate all areas of their lives on a scale of feeling overwhelmed to empowered. Any areas that show up on the overwhelmed side of the scale are often dealt with first.

Liza scored her environment very low, as she was felt overwhelmed at home. She felt like she spent all her free time cleaning. She also reported having very low energy in addition to stomach issues. In the afternoons of her days off, if no one were home, she would take a nap for a couple of hours.

The home office she shared with her fiancé was filled with clutter, which mad her anxious, so she asked if we could start there. Liza felt disorganized and behind in her bills. Every time she attempted to start going through some boxes, she would get overwhelmed, stop, and go lay down. Although she knew the office needed attention, she was ashamed to have me over to help her out. She repeatedly apologized for having me come help although she was paying me for my service.

When I arrived, I walked along the hallway slowly and could see through the doorway that the room was crammed full. There were boxes of stuff stacked on the floor; overflowing bookshelves; desks and chairs were covered in paper; toys all over the floor; and tons of knickknacks. The air was stagnant.

What initially started with a few extra boxes shoved into the office before guests arrived for a dinner, quickly developed into a dumping ground over the next couple of years for everything and everyone in the house, Liza explained. You couldn't walk across the room without stepping on something.

The first thing we did was open the window to bring fresh air in the room. When I announced that it was time to get rid of some clutter, sheer panic crossed Liza's face. You would have thought I had told her to get rid of her first-born child. She was adamant that there were things of sentimental value she wanted to keep. When she was a teenager, she lost her childhood home--and all of her possessions--to a fire. As we sifted through her things, it became apparent that she had not thrown anything out since then.

The first area we tackled were her medical books from school. It had been more than 15 years since she had graduated yet she had kept all her textbooks, notes, tests, reports, and binders full of handouts. All of this stuff was taking up over half an overstuffed bookcase. When I mentioned that it might be time to get rid of some it, she became short of breath and a little sweaty. She wanted to keep it--*all* of it. So, we sat down and talked it out.

"When was the last time you opened any of the books?" I asked her.

"I haven't since I left school," she replied.

"Do you think that perhaps in the past 15 years there have been medical advances that would make some of the information in these books outdated?"

"Yes...."

"How do you currently research a medical question?"

"I discuss it with a colleague or on search the Internet."

"So, you're telling me you will never use any of this again?"

"Ummmm . . . Yes."

"So, why do you want to keep it?"

Her number one reason was, "Just in case I need it." Obviously, in the past 15 years she had never once needed it. The "just-in-case" mindset is a fear-based mentality that says you do not believe in the future. It says that we do not believe the universe will provide for us. We do not believe that _we_ can provide for _ourselves_. It puts us into a mindset of poverty versus prosperity. With that mindset, you've already lost before you have begun. If you truly think you will need it and you throw it away, you will definitely need it in some obscure way. But, if you think and recognize this does not serve me now so I will let it go, you are freed to fearlessly embrace the future and allow it to provide for you what you do need at the right time.

Her second reason to keep everything was that graduating from school was a symbol of a tough period in her life that she had conquered. While in school, she had overdosed on drugs and nearly died. Despite all the chaos in her personal life, she made it through college and graduated with honors. That is an impressive feat to be very proud of. However, that period in her life was bitter sweet. A lot of really bad things happened during that time. The problem with keeping all this stuff was it brought her back to a dark period in her life. While it did symbolize success and achievement, she could not look at it without also thinking how crappy of a time it was. She did not like who she was back then. Her stuff kept her living in the past, when in reality, after 15 years, she was a completely different person doing many great things. The past kept her being small. It told her, "You are a no-good druggy that will never amount to much." As much as she was tried to make positive changes in her life, she kept getting sucked back a few steps and it taken a toll on her health and potential to become even more successful.

After our discussion, she was willing to let things go slowly. We took photographs with her smart phone of any memento from college that was significant to her like a high grade on an especially challenging paper, pins she had earned, etc. She felt good about having the photos to look back on if she felt inclined to do so. As we continued to go through everything, she gained more confidence to let things go. It was hard, but she did it. As she continued to clear her space, the process grew easier and easier.

The next area we attacked was her knickknacks, which were on shelves, on her desk, fallen behind the bookcase--they were everywhere. One of the things she had initially complained about was the fact she spent so much of her free time cleaning. No wonder! Knickknacks take a lot of time to take care of. They collect dust, get dirty, and they're small so it takes extra effort to handle them. Who has time for that? A lot of people like to collect things, but a small interest can quickly spiral out of control and become overwhelming. Instead of knickknacks enhancing our environments and making them more beautiful, they can create clutter and visual chaos and confusion.

As I looked through all the knickknacks, it slowly dawned on me that they were all related to the ocean. She had seashells, dolphins, whales, sea glass, and boats. I asked her why was everything related to the ocean? Liza said that she loved the water and it was her dream to retire and live by the ocean. Mind you, Liza was about 30 years away from retirement. I asked her why she didn't live by the water now, instead of the mountains where she currently resided. She gave me several reasons that kept her from moving to her dream location. It never occurred to her that she could do it now rather than when she retired. That simple, self-limiting thought had kept her from doing something to increase her happiness and wellbeing. However, that she hired me proved that she was ready to receive help, which is an important component of any desire for progress. Our conversation about the possibility of moving was what she needed at that moment. Life was already nudging her in that direction. How many knickknacks was it going to take? I think she was lucky it was only about 20 years' worth!

Like the textbooks, Liza resisted doing away with the knickknacks. She'd say, "I can't get rid of that, so and so gave it to me. They would be so mad if I got rid of it." This a prime example of falling into the trap of guilt and obligation, which are two things that can wreak havoc on the most well-intentioned life. When you allow someone else to dictate your decisions, you give up control of your life to them. This is also another example of fear-based living. When an item brought up guilt and obligation, I would ask, "Do you love it?" The answer was always "No." The object was the wrong color, broken, not her style, ugly, and on and on.

"Why keep these things?" I asked again.

"Oh, she will be so angry if I get rid of it," Liza responded.

"Ok, has she been in this room recently to see the item?"

"No."

"When was this given to you?"

"I don't remember."

"Do you even like this person?"

"Not really."

At some point in our lives, we have probably given a gift with the best intentions but it was completely wrong for the intended person. If they didn't like it, would you be insulted if they got rid of it? The answer would most likely be no. If you loved them and wanted only the best for them, you would want them to love what you had given them instead of holding on to something out of obligation. Keeping things we do not love around us brings us down and lowers our energy. If you keep things from people you don't particularly like, it is even worse. Keeping the object lets that person have control over your life and holds you in the past. Guilt manifests from the inside. You have the choice to decide whether or not something will make you feel bad. It is ok to say, "I have changed and this gift no longer works for me." Or frankly, "I have never liked this object and it is time to let it go." It is ok to admit it. It is very important to be honest with yourself. You put other people ahead of yourself when you make decisions based on what you think they may feel. Without asking them, do you even know that is what they think? How is that fair to you? You are stuck with an object you hate and bitter someone has control over your emotions, which forces you to live in the past. Life is too short to be worried by things and situations that don't exist. Let it go!

I saw Liza again a few weeks later and the first thing she did was thank me for giving her permission to get rid of things. I reminded her that she did the work and to own it and that I just gave her a little nudge. She told me that she realized a lot of her decisions in life were based on obligation. The second thing she reported was that she was on a roll! Liza had gone through her whole office and had begun to make her way through the rest of the house. She felt invigorated and full of energy. She had stopped taking the mid-afternoon naps and was excited to go through all her belongings. Liza noted that she was motivated to purge things from her home because she would have less to pack when she was ready to move--something she had never thought she would want to do but was now excited about. She felt like a heavy load had been lifted from her. It had felt good to get rid of things that reminded her of when she was depressed and in a dark place. Liza was happy to report that she didn't miss anything. She looked great. Her eyes were brighter and her skin looked healthier. You could tell she had lost a few pounds. For the first time in many years, she was excited for new possibilities and opportunities to enter into her life. The best part was she now fearlessly embraced these changes and took control of her life. Liza now dictated what would happen in her life instead of letting life happen to her.

The one thing she continued to repeat was, "I can't believe I had been keeping all this stuff for so many years!"

At this point, you can see there are a lot of reasons why we do keep things we don't need. The most important thing to keep in mind is that you are not your possessions. What you own is not your love, kindness, generosity, success, beauty, happiness, health, and well-being.

Daily, we are bombarded by companies that spend billions in marketing to encourage us to want the biggest, best, newest, thing to hit the shelves. Status and success are measured by what job you have, how much you own, how expensive your car is, how big your house is, and how fancy your clothes are.

There is no doubt that we all love to own things. The want created by these companies can make people strive for a better lifestyle. However, how that lifestyle is measured is relative and objects do not make us truly happy or successful. It is often the pursuit of acquiring the object or the symbol of what it stands for that create the feelings around it.

How many times have you wanted something so badly and after you bought it you felt a little down? Perhaps you even used it for a short time and then forgot about it. We are in a time where we can buy anything we want at any time of day. Things are mass produced and cheaply made. Have you ever been outside a box store and seen people pushing shopping carts full of junk to their cars? "It was on sale, so I bought three!" they exclaim. When things are acquired without thought, care, or to fill an emotional void, they weigh us down and create clutter.

We are marketed to think that we are the objects we buy. I hate to break it to you, but you entered this world with nothing and you will leave it with nothing. You were a person before you could buy or acquire anything for yourself.

As a designer, I believe in the power of well-designed objects. They can enhance our lives and increase the beauty around us. I'm not advocating that you should live like a monk. I am saying that you should be very aware of the objects you bring into your home and know when it is time to let them go. Some objects serve us for a while and then don't. Things change. We change.

Exercise:

Keeping in mind that you are not your possessions, open your journal. Take 10 minutes to reflect on the following questions:

- What do you value in life? Is it health, kindness, money, love, etc.?

- What is your favorite thing that you own? Why? What would you do if you no longer had it? How would you feel?

CLEAR

Ten

Getting Rid Of Clutter

Are you ready to get clear? Are you ready to simplify your life, set yourself free, feel lighter, inspired, and live fearlessly?

Whether you live in an 80 sq foot bedroom in your parent's home or in a 10,000 sq foot mansion, you can benefit from dealing with clutter. No matter where or how you live, it is time for your habitat to become a reflection of your healthy well-being and be a space where you feel love, inspiration, and creativity to design and live the life you want.

Getting rid of clutter is an intense experience. Make sure you are in a place in your life where you are one hundred percent sure you want to do this. If you feel any apprehension, wait until you are whole-heartedly ready. Keep in mind, there is a difference between apprehension and fear. We are here to break habits and live from a place of empowerment. Always listen to what your gut tells you. If you have read the book to this point, you probably have already committed to making changes to your environment and life. So, let's get started.

Where To Start

It is easiest to break up your environment into sections. Start in an area you feel you will benefit from the most. You can start with a junk drawer, the top of your desk, or your whole kitchen. This is your personal experience; make this as big or small of an effort as you want. No matter how much or little you take on, you will experience a shift in your life. At the very least, you will feel good after it's done. It's time to be fearless and dig right in!

Be aware that sorting through your clutter may bring up emotions or memories you have not experienced in a while. You may be surprised at how you react to certain things. Remember not to judge yourself or give up. You will be greatly rewarded once you are done.

Since this may be an emotionally and physically exhausting, be cognizant to practice self-care throughout. Make sure you drink plenty of water during day and get a full night's sleep. If you are working on a room, take frequent breaks to get up and stretch. Make sure to exercise. Taking a long leisure walk at the end of a full day will help you wind down, allow you the time to reflect on your experience, and clear your mind. Since clutter is stagnant energy, you will benefit from a walk in the fresh air. If you are able to open up windows while working in a room, do it. If you choose to play music while working, make sure to play something that is upbeat and inspiring. Avoid any music that reminds you of a soured relationship or a bad time in your life. Wear clothes that fit and allow you to move loosely; you should unafraid for them to get dirty or be torn. Make sure to have plenty of heavy duty garbage bags ready, empty boxes to place things in to move, a set of gloves and small tools like screw drivers if applicable.

Do not clear anyone else's clutter without their permission. Especially if your relationship is on the fritz, this could have a devastating effect. You will see that through your actions of clearing your clutter, people around you will naturally start to clear their own clutter without prompting. If they don't, it may shed clarity on a situation you have previously been unable to understand.

Before you begin to work, set an intention that best fits your reason for doing this. One you might like to try is:

> Dear Divine Power, please give me the strength to face my fears and guide me to create a space that is reflective of my love and light.

Be prepared, because once you get going, you will find yourself obsessed with getting rid of clutter!

Areas To Clear

Entryway

There is a lot that can collect where we enter or leave a building. It can be an official dumping ground for everything you bring into the house or intend to take out. Since we spend so little time in entryways, we often overlook all the stuff we have dropped there. These areas tend to be on the smaller side. If they are not well organized, they can create a lot of confusion, wasted time, and distress. Why would you want to experience that every time you leave or enter your home? Your entryway is your first and last connection to your home. It sets the tone for the rest of your experience both inside and outside of the home.

You should be able to open and close all doors fully and easily. There should not be any obstructions behind the doors to block them, such as coats hanging on hooks or shoes wedged at the bottom. Remove anything that has collected on the floor around entrances and exits, or down hallways. Keys should have once place to go. Go through key trays. If you do not know what a key belongs to, throw it out. Make sure all umbrellas work and get rid of any extras; you do not need more than one umbrella per person. Go through the coat rack and see if there is anything you haven't worn in the past 6 months. Sift through drawers of any furniture in that area. Make sure to clear behind and under all furniture.

Kitchen

Kitchens are often considered the heart of the home. They are where we go for nourishment and community. If you hate to cook or have health issues, a lot can be linked to the state of your kitchen. Is it clean? Do you have a space to work? Is the lighting good? Do your cabinets overflow? Do all the drawers close properly? Do you have basic cooking utensils? Is your food fresh? When we make changes in our diet or feel like we are stuck at a weight loss plateau, our kitchens can be in complete disarray. Is your kitchen used to improve your wellbeing or do you use it as an office? Do you feel completely overwhelmed when you look in your fridge, such that you eat out all the time?

A good place to start clearing is the refrigerator and freezer. This is the lifeline to your health. If your refrigerator is a mess, most likely your diet is too. Throw out anything you cannot identify. Check all dates on condiments and remove anything that is expired or has freezer burn. Organize your refrigerator and freezer and make sure that neither is crammed full. You should be able to easily sort through everything to find what you need to cook.

Check the tops of cabinets and work down through all the cabinets and drawers. If you haven't used something in the past 6 months, you probably don't need it. Throw out all expired food. Make sure to check all spices, supplements, and medications. Spices should be no more than one year old. If you can't remember when you bought something, chuck it. Go through all your canned goods. If you haven't made anything with that can of condensed milk that you got on sale a few months back, donate it. If you have a collection of mismatched mugs, glasses, or plates, consider giving them away. Although you think they may be quaint and kitschy, they create chaos in the cabinets. Matching dinnerware creates a calm rhythm on your shelves. You do not need any more distractions in your life. The same goes for collections of vases, spoons, etc. Get rid of anything that is chipped or broken. Consider whether or not you need more than one type an item such as vegetable peelers? All your knives should be sharp.

All your appliances should be in working order. If you have any appliances that you haven't used in the past 6 months, donate them. A good example is juicers. Maybe you went through a phase where you used it for a month, but it has been collecting dust for the past 2 years. Every time you look at it, you feel guilty and think you should be juicing but you never do. Get rid of it. You don't need anything in your life to make you feel guilty. If you ever do decide to get into juicing again, you can buy one then, but in the meantime, you can use that gained space. Make sure to go through closets, pantries, and under sinks. You do not need to keep every plastic bag you acquire from shopping.

All your furniture should be stable and functional. If you have any chairs with torn seats or wobbly legs, either get them fixed or say goodbye. Have a comfortable place to sit while you eat. Standing up at your counter while you scarf your food shows little respect for your body and the nourishment you consume. Remove TVs from kitchen. When you eat, focus on eating and conversing with the other people at the table.

When you watch TV or surf the net while you eat, you unknowingly eat too fast and have the tendency to over eat. Watching the news and melodramas can cause negativity, which may cause you to swallow those emotions with your food.

Bathrooms

Is your countertop covered with various beauty products? Do you have collections of empty perfume bottles? Does your medicine cabinet close all the way? We spend a lot of time in bathrooms and they are a place for you to focus on your self-care. If you feel stressed out every morning because you're constantly knocking things off your counter while getting ready for work, it's time to lighten the load.

Go through all cabinets, shower, closets, and areas under the sink. Check all expiration dates on medicines and beauty products. If you haven't worn that color of eye shadow in the past 6 months, toss it. If you have a lot of bottles with a little bit of product at the bottom of them, let them go. Check the shower for these lingering bottles. Go through all linens and towels. If anything is frayed, worn or has a hole in it, it either gets thrown out or put in the rag bin (which should be kept small). Check that all appliances work, such as hair dryers, electric shavers or toothbrushes, curling irons, etc. You do not need to keep outdated hair accessories like scrunchies. Consider how many decorative soaps or hand towels you really need.

Closets

Out of sight and out of mind is hazardous to your health. If you keep shoving things into closets so you don't have to immediately deal with them, you will build a mountain of issues to deal with later. The same goes in your life. Remember, your environment reflection of your life. If you keep your closets clean and organized with plenty of free space, it says a lot about your mindset and current place in life.

Make sure to go through every single closet. Try on all clothes. If something doesn't fit right, is the wrong color or pattern, get rid of it. You should love every item of clothing you buy. Many people purchase items because they are on sale or from cheap stores. Your clothes are a reflection of your personal taste and style. It is better to own fewer well-made items that you love and make you feel powerful than closets full of crappy clothes that you don't feel good in. Do not keep clothes that you no longer fit. If you gained weight and hope to someday get back into those five pairs of jeans, stop torturing yourself and let them go. Keeping them keeps you living in your past.

Don't save things to hand down to your children. If you aren't going to give it to them right now, get rid of it. If you think that you should hold onto something because it might come back into fashion, get rid of it. You will never wear it and 25 from now, you'll look silly trying to rock it. Go through all shoes. If they are worn, have holes, or you haven't used them in the past year, see ya later. Do the same with all accessories. How many baseball hats do you need? Go through all boxes, and every shelf.

Living Area

Your living room, den, media room, or any area you would spend a lot of time in should be welcoming and easy to navigate. These are rooms you should be able to entertain in or spend quiet time alone.

Go through all furniture in these rooms. Check drawers, cabinets, under and behind pieces of furniture. Coffee tables should be clear and usable. Limit the amount of knickknacks and magazines or books on surfaces. Go through all DVD and game collections. People love to showcase their collections in these common rooms. Make sure the collection is relevant to your current life. If you amassed glass figurines of ballerinas as a child, but no longer dance or watch ballets, do you still need them? Make sure to pay attention to all the wires in these rooms. It shouldn't look like a jumbled mess behind the TV. Organize the cords so they neatly layout and you can tell which electronic they lead to. Make sure furniture is comfortable and that pillows are fluffy and look fresh. If anything is broken or worn, get rid of it.

Bedrooms

A good night's sleep is imperative to living a healthy life. Your bedroom should be a calming oasis free of clutter and stress. Less is more when it comes to bedrooms. People often overstuff the rooms with too much furniture and junk. Your bedroom should have the least amount of furniture possible. Avoid keeping anything under your bed, except for linens and extra blankets, if necessary. Own a proper alarm clock that works. Do not use your phone as an alarm or not sleep with your phone on your nightstand. Your phone should spend the night charging in another room. Keep your home office out of your room. Your bedroom is for sleep and intimacy, not work. Your pillows should be changed every 2 years. If they are flat and feel heavy, get rid of them. Pillows collect dust mites and dander over time, which is super gross and unhealthy. Try to change your bed sheets weekly.

You should be able to walk across your room without stepping on clothes, papers, or anything else. Go through all wardrobes and furniture. Check drawers, behind and under furniture. Go through jewelry cases and get rid of pieces that are broken, single earrings without matches, or any cheap pieces you haven't worn in over a year. Check how much you own of one thing. If you have 20 belts, you probably don't need all of them. Go through everything on the top surface of the dressers.

Dining Room

There has been a decline in the use of dining rooms. A lot of modern homes do not even have them. If you live in a house that has one, try to use it daily instead of on special occasions or as a showpiece room or the room that collects junk from the kitchen. The separation of where we eat from where we cook is a beautiful thing. A dining room allows you to focus on eating and conversation. It makes your dining experience special. Honoring your meal and enjoying the company of guests or family will greatly enhance your life.

Go through all pieces of furniture. Make sure the china cabinet is organized. Get rid of any dishes that are chipped or broken. Make sure sets are complete. For instance, if you have a sugar bowl with a missing lid or creamer, let it go. Clear beneath and behind all furniture. Look through tablecloths and napkins. If anything is worn, torn, or frayed, get rid of it. Go through all collections of dishes, figurines, etc. How many pieces of fake fruits do you need in the centerpiece bowl?

Office/Workspaces

Whether at home or in the workplace, clearing your desk or workspace will have a profound effect. Is the top of your desk covered with paperwork? A cluttered workspace leads to lethargy, procrastination, sloppy work, and overwhelm. When your desk is organized and you have an open space to work, you can think clearly and work efficiently. It is very empowering to do work you are proud of. This allows for inspiration and creativity to enter into your life and gives you bold ideas to be more successful.

As a reflection of your life, a messy desk, cubicle, or office can have an incredibly negative affect on how people view you at your company. If you wish to get a promotion or be viewed as a leader within your organization, you should take serious a look at what state your desk is in. You may have the best intentions, but your desk could say a lot of things about you such as, "I have no attention to detail. I don't value other people's property or work. I'm disorganized. I'm distracted and waste a lot of time." Some of the biggest disputes between colleagues are the cleanliness of shared spaces. Don't be the person to cause fights over disarray.

Keep the personal memorabilia or collections at home. Do you want to be known as the person with the desk full of pug pictures or do you want to be known as Jane or John who just killed the presentation for the new account? People always talk about the messiest offices. Don't let your environment outshine your work.

When clearing your office, go through all file cabinets. Sort through all papers. Get rid of anything you haven't looked at in a year and tax info older than 7 years. Don't keep scrap paper to write notes on. It is messy, unorganized, and you'll never look at them. Put notes in a notebook or use a smart phone app to capture them. All those pens you have collected over the years? Throw them out and buy two new ones. Do you have a bunch of free tchotchkes from tradeshows you have attended? All those useless toys and stress balls with company logos on them create unnecessary clutter. Throw them out.

Do you have photos, saved tickets from shows you have attended, or random inspirational images pinned around the office? Pare down the images and make sure they are relevant to who and where you are today. You don't need old memories that keep you in the past. Get rid of multiples of things you don't need, such as calculators and calendars. You shouldn't store anything under your desk. Go through every surface, cabinet, and drawer. If you don't know where to put something, than you don't need it. Your chair should be comfortable. If it rolls, it should do so freely.

Books can cause a lot of clutter. You may hold on to them because you like having them around you. But books can cause stagnation. As your interests change over the years, your library should reflect that. When your shelves are stuffed, it doesn't allow for new ideas or thoughts to enter into your life. Growth occurs when we continue to learn and keep our minds open.

Garage

Garages were made to hold cars, not all the junk you don't want in your house. They become great dumping grounds for all the leftover bits and parts of projects, miscellaneous things we don't know what to do with, and things we want to forget about. If you cannot park your car in your garage, it is time to consider making room so that you can. A clean and well-organized garage gives you space to work on projects more efficiently and will cut down on all the time you waste going through boxes looking for the one thing you need and swear you kept. You can always bet, after searching for it for too long, you'll give up and go buy a new one of it anyway, adding to the overall clutter.

Since garages can be overwhelming with the sheer volume of stuff we can fit into them, take your time and be realistic about how much can be done in a day. As with all the other rooms, anything broken or worn should be let go. If you have multiples of anything, assess how many of the same item you need. Old car parts, leftover cans of paint, and miscellaneous nails and screws can all be let go. If you live in a climate with humidity, let go of things that have mildew which can cause health issues and attract bugs. Ditch any items from old unfinished projects you haven't completed for the past 5 years. You can sell the parts and if you find yourself ready to return to the project in the future, you will be able to attract all the things you need at that time to make it happen.

Basements/Attics

Conflicted with the same issues as garages, basements and attics become dumping grounds for all the things we do not want to deal with. Because these areas tend to be wet or very hot, a lot of things stored in these areas disintegrate over time. It is important to go through these areas yearly, not only to clear clutter but also to make sure bugs and pests are not hiding within your clutter.

Storage Sheds

Resist the urge to buy storage sheds to hide clutter. They often become places to park broken lawn equipment, and everything you can't fit in your garage. Do you really need all the items that warrant a shed?

Porches/Patios

Often used as an extension of the home, porches can collect a lot of clutter. Not only can they hold outdoor furniture, grills, and plants, they can also become cluttered with debris and fallen leaves.

Clean these areas regularly to bringing positive energy around the home. Make sure to deal with any dead plants in these areas. Get rid of planters, lawn ornaments, and furniture that are broken or worn.

Cars

We spend a lot of time in our cars, so they naturally reflect the state of our life. If you are embarrassed to have anyone in your car, there are some issues to be dealt with. If you can't fit anyone else into your car because there is too much clutter inside, it's definitely time for a clearing. There is no need to have a garbage bag in your car. When you get out of your car, take all your garbage with you. If you remove garbage immediately and daily, it won't become an issue. I recommend making a rule of no eating in the car. Sounds crazy, I know. Consider this: When you eat in your car you do yourself a disservice. If you want to achieve health and fitness goals, this action can cause you to gain weight. Eating while driving leads to mindless munching, overeating, and indigestion as you rush to finish your food. It also creates a mess and no one wants to show up somewhere with a stain on their pants.

Purses/baggage/wallets/pockets

Although these areas may be small--with the exception of most purses--they can harbor a lot of clutter. Going through these areas regularly will help lighten the load--figuratively and mentally-- that you carry around, which will reduce back and neck pain and mental anguish. How many lip- glosses do you need at one time? Do you keep old receipts? How many pairs of shoes do you need for a three-day trip? Can the change be used? These are areas that are susceptible to the "just-in-case" mentality. At this point in time, you can go buy anything you might need on a whim. This is especially important to keep in mind with traveling. There are plenty of box stores available to purchase an item you left at home. The lighter you travel, the more likely you are to have an unexpected adventure. These experiences can lead to tremendous growth in our lives.

తొందిగ

Remember that when you clear, you can make this work as big or small as you want. You may find that you want to start small with a junk drawer and work your way up to the whole garage. Wherever you are, just start. The above outline is intended to help guide you through the process of clearing. There are no hard and fast rules on how to do this, just as there are no rules on how to live your life. The goal is to create a space that reflects your healthiest, most vibrant self. Being fearless and getting rid of clutter will allow for you to shine from within your surroundings.

Part Three

Surrounded By Beauty

Eleven

What Is Beautiful?

I once had a rambunctious, green-eye-shadowed, 90-something client named Gert who has since passed away. Gert had an appraiser from Sotheby's come to her house to value furniture and art she'd spent 60-plus years collecting. The gentleman said, "You have a good eye." To which she responded, "Which one?"

This sassy response was typical of Gert. We spent a lot of time together to rework her home after she'd been forced to remodel due to damage from a burst pipe. During that time, we had a lot of great conversations. While I helped her with her home, she imparted to me a lot of wisdom from her many years of life. She told me that when she went back to work after her children were grown, she made it her goal to make enough money to buy whatever piece of clothing she wanted so she could wear it to any type of event ever imagined-- from the Kentucky Derby to a glitzy gala event. This goal lead Gert to go back to school in her 40s to re-imagine her life. She made a lot of money up until her death because she loved her work and life. The simple goal of acquiring beautiful clothing drove her to become more successful and to create a life she loved.

"Beauty is in the eye of the beholder."

Everyone has probably heard this saying at some point. It's so well known because it is absolutely true. Beauty is subjective. How we look at things and perceive them is personal and also cultural. Two people can see the same painting and take away two completely different impressions of it.

When I was in design school, my roommate Kerry and I went to the MoMA NYC for a school assignment. We stood in front of an Abstract

Expressionist painting from artist Agnes Martin. This particular artist is known for his paintings that often depict lines. Kerry and I discussed the merits of this painting in relation to the era it was made and the assignment guidelines. We both were in accord that it was beautiful. The nuances of the lines were delicate and colors were arresting. Although this is what we felt, we also tried to sound smart and articulate as would be expected in our report. Realistically, we probably sounded a tad obnoxious in way that only 20-year-old art students can. As the discussion continued, we noticed a gentleman to our left standing a little too close, leaning in towards us. I turned to him and asked "Hey, what do you think of this painting?"

"I was trying to hear what you were saying because to me this looks like someone trying to paint graph paper," he replied. "Why would you do that when you can buy it from a store? The lines would be a hell of a lot straighter!"

Several museum patrons "shushed" us as our uncontrolled laughter shook the quiet gallery. We did try to convince the gentleman of our view. However, he was totally right and so were we. Beauty *is* in the eye of the beholder.

From a visual standpoint, we can be influenced by styles that come into fashion or that are relevant to a specific time period. This is illustrated in how we dress, the cars we drive, and how our houses are decorated. While some design styles are timeless, many are fleeting.

We can be influenced culturally. Where we grow up may dictate what type of things we may be attracted to. As a first generation American, I attracted other first generation Americans as friends. We used to collectively joke about the different styles our families sported. My Dominican friend always made fun of the plastic rug runners and covers on the 'nice' couches while my Sri Lankan friend would question how many naked booby Hindi statues a house really needed to have. Those cultural styles and ideas of beauty can only really be understood by the culture from which they come.

Beauty can be found in a moment where all things come together in the right way. For example, your version of beauty might be a football game in which the perfect play leads to a winning goal at the last second. Everything aligns perfectly for a victory. This can also be related to kismet--without prompting or explanation, things come together perfectly.

Beauty can be something that you feel on a visceral level. This might come in the form of a sleeping lover or a child deep in play. You may come across a flower and it might strike you as the most beautiful thing you have seen all week.

When you come across something that you find beautiful, you know it right away. You feel a surge of energy and emotion. You get a little excited and your heart rate quickens. Take, for instance, when you come across a beautiful sunset or you see an exotic, well-designed car, or hear a piece of music that brought you to tears. How did those experiences make you feel?

When you get right down to it, *beauty makes us feel good.* And the great thing about beauty is that there is no wrong way to perceive it. You are in complete control of what you find beautiful, and being able to recognize it when you see it can change your life.

Beauty reinforces positive feelings. If you are having a bad day and it feels like the whole world is against you, you might happen to catch a glimpse of a gorgeous sunset that reminds you that life is good. It's hard to ignore the power of the beauty when you are in awe. In that moment, it is difficult to say life sucks when it is apparent that there are some gifts from the universe that are pretty amazing. Beauty inspires us to be better. When you see something that is beautiful, you become hopeful and inspired. Maybe it is something you want to own like a beautifully detailed Italian leather purse, or you see something you want to do, such as climb Machu Picchu. Beauty can lead you on a quest toward self-improvement so you can accomplish a feat or afford a desired object. The inspiration leads to increased success because you change your life in positive ways to make it happen.

In the following exercise, take a look at the areas within your environment that you find beautiful and those that are not. This is the first step to developing a healthy surrounding filled with beauty.

Exercise:

Take your journal and find a place in your home that you consider beautiful. Sit and get comfortable. Bring your attention to the room. Take several deep breaths in through your nose and out through your mouth. Open your journal. Write a list of all the things you find beautiful in this area. Describe the way the makes you feel, what you see; include the details, and the smells.

Record your observations without judging them.

Once you are finished, find an area in your home that you don't like and get as comfortable as you can. Slow your breathing, and become aware of what you are looking at. Open your journal and make a list. What do you hate about it? How does it make you feel? What does it look like? What is the light like? How does it smell? With as much detail as possible, record all your observations without judging them.

Now that you know what you find beautiful and what you do not like in your surroundings, are you ready to allow beauty into your life?

Twelve

Letting Beauty Into Your Life

For all the things that we let into our lives and environments, how many of them do we consider beautiful? In the "Clutter" section of this book, you did the work to fearlessly clear your surroundings of the things that bog you down. There is a lot of emotion that comes with letting go of the things in our lives that do not currently serve us. The work that you have done or will do makes room to allow more success in your life and to live your life in a way that best reflects the intentions and goals you have for yourself.

As hard as it is to let things go, it is equally hard to let things *in* to our lives. A lot of people won't even try to acquire or be surrounded by beautiful things because they feel they are unworthy of it. It may not be a conscious decision, but it is reflected in their surroundings and how they treat themselves. When you let beauty into your life, it reflects that you value yourself and honor your surroundings. You feel that you are worthy to receive this beauty.

Consider my former client, Julia, who was a successful sales executive. From the outside world perspective, she had it going on. She was smart, business savvy, had a six-figure income, and traveled the world. Each year, she would receive her earned bonus and save it so that she could buy a house. While that sounds like a great financial plan and a smart use of her money, there was a problem. Julia had been saving for a home for more than 15 years and had yet to buy one. In addition to the house, she had also lusted after a Cartier watch for many years. Every few months, Julia would talk about that watch. She'd say something like, "When I buy my house, then I'll be able to buy my watch." Or, "After this year is done and I get my next bonus, then I'll be able to buy my watch." Although she had enough savings to afford both the house and the watch, she made excuses as to why she would have to wait to buy either.

One day during a session as the watch came up yet again, I used the opportunity to dig deeper. When I asked her what she loved so much about the watch, she mentioned that it was the design that first caught her eye. After lusting for it for 5 years, she still loved it as much as the first time saw it. She admitted that as she traveled into different cities, if she had the time she would find a Cartier store and try it on.

As I continued to dig, I learned that she felt the watch symbolized that she had made it in life. She wasn't so concerned about the name brand of the watch, but she appreciated how finely made it was and how the diamonds lit up in the light. She felt like a successful woman wearing it. When I pointed out that she *was* a successful woman, she started to cry. Julia lamented that she didn't feel like she was successful at all. She didn't feel she was the type of person who deserved to own such fine jewelry. In fact, she was scared that if she bought the watch she would fall into financial ruin and have to sell it.

It took Julia a while to work through these fear-based thoughts. She started the healing process when she was able to admit out loud what the watch meant to her. By speaking the words, she consciously became aware of how she viewed and treated herself. Although she was abundant in her wealth, she desperately lacked self worth. At the end of our coaching, Julia awarded herself with the purchase of the watch. She celebrated that she was on a journey to become more successful. To do that, she needed to acknowledge that she was worthy of all good things to come into her life. By allowing the beauty of the watch into her life, she honored herself and opened the door for greater feelings of happiness and self worth.

I ran into Julia recently, who wore her gorgeous watch. Not only did she look great, she also told me that she was renovating a charming house in the Hudson Valley of New York. She was proud to report that life was good and she had just celebrated a promotion by going to Iceland for a vacation.

Personal Appearance and Self-Worth

Another example of resisting beauty can be found in the office. Have you ever worked with someone who refuses to wear nice office-appropriate clothes because they say they don't care what society thinks; they are exerting their personality, and if you don't like it, too bad? I'm all for being a rebel. But, what this person doesn't realize is that when he wears worn, ill-fitting clothes, it says that he doesn't believe in himself and has low self-esteem. When you present yourself that way, you lose your respect and power. People do not take you seriously even if you are the best at what you do. This is fear-based living. By trying to deflect the attention away from you with excuses, you are afraid of living in the light. You don't have to dress sloppily to exude individuality. You can be well dressed and still show your individual expression.

We play these games with ourselves all the time. We think we're making a decision or a stance, and then we don't realize that it actually comes off in a different way.

The same happens within your environment. By ignoring or unconsciously being unaware of your surroundings or how you look, you let your environment reflect parts of you that you don't want to highlight. In that offhand, dismissive way that we can have with our clothes or with the things we own, we invite all sorts of negative energy into our lives.

Part of letting beauty into your life is to treat your belongings with care and respect. When you do, you also treat yourself the same way. That is fearless living that allows you the ability to be more successful. Objects and things that are whole, clean, respected, and well maintained are far more beautiful than ones that are treated with carelessness, distain, and hate. When you do not treat yourself with care or respect, you live from a place of fear.

The Façade of Beauty

Beauty can also be used with the wrong intention. Have you ever met someone who is obsessed with having the most "magazine perfect" home or lusciously manicured lawn or symmetrical nose? This pursuit of beauty is really idealism and reaches into the realm of perfection, which is not the same as surrounding yourself with beauty. Although related, the reasons behind the two could not be more different.

When someone pursues beauty in a fanatical way, such as spending thousands spent on plastic surgery, the outcome might seem beautiful, but it comes at the cost of happiness. This mindset makes it so beauty can never be attained because there will always be a fault, and a continued obsession to fix it. Frankly, this leads to a pretty miserable life. It is the opposite action of using clutter to cover up your not worthiness, but the outcome is the same. It will cause a state of living negatively in a beautiful place that will not be seen or appreciated. The goal is to enhance your life and surround yourself in beauty that is real to *you*, not to any other outside influence or standard. Being able to do that is living fearlessly. You choose yourself over any outside influence.

Some people may say, "I know I have no taste so I'm not sure how to let beauty into my life because I don't even know what it is." This is just an excuse that comes from fear. As you learned in the previous chapter, beauty comes from individual perspective. When you use the words "taste" or "style," you refer to a *form* of beauty that is always subjective. If you make decisions based on what feels right to you, you can never go wrong. There is no right way to do this and for each person it will be an individual experience. The point is now that you have cleared the space of clutter it is time to allow beauty to come in. With beauty comes harmony, balance, strength and all the things you need to live fearlessly.

Exercise:

Do you allow beauty into your life? Take your journal. At the beginning of *Clear*, you were asked to choose a journal that you love the look and physical feel of. Did you choose one that fits this description, or did you settle for a random journal you already had in the house? Take 10 minutes and answer the following questions:

- Is there anything of beauty that you want but will not let into your life? Why?

- Do you feel you can now take the steps to let that beauty in? What would it take to make it happen?

CLEAR

Thirteen

How Do You Want Your Life To Be?

Your environment is a reflection of your life. Knowing that, what would you like your environment to say about you? You are the only one who has control over your life. As such, you have the control to create the home and work space that aligns with your highest vision. That you are reading this book means you have either decided to start making changes in your life or you have actively begun making changes.

I love how fearless you are being in deciding to change.

The Victim Mindset

It takes a lot of courage and self-reflection to change your life. You first have to recognize that the way things currently are, aren't serving you. Although many of us know deep down when things aren't optimal, we can often ignore the situation or feelings around and inside us. When Sofi came to me, she wanted help with her binge eating. Overall, she was pretty healthy from the outside. She ate all the right foods and worked out regularly. The problem was that Sofi would secretly binge at night, a few times a week, when she came home from work. She described her binging as stuffing her emotions. When she binged, she would eat peanut butter out of the jar and mentally check out. She described that she felt separated from her body when she went into her binge trance. When she came to, she would feel stuffed and ashamed of her actions.

Sofi recognized that this pattern wasn't helping her in life. She finally sought help to change this behavior as she had been doing this for over fifteen years. One thing that became apparent while we worked together is that Sofi blamed everyone and anything for what happened in her life. She was a pro at being a victim. She hated her job and blamed it on her boss. She hated her house and blamed it on her husband. She was always late and blamed it on her dogs. Sofi never took responsibility for her actions. Even when she was binging and physically putting the food in her mouth herself, she blamed it on being tired. What does being tired have to do with eating too much? Sofi ignored what was the root cause of her problem in life. She was living passively as a victim. It took time and reflection to change Sofi's mindset. When she started to own her actions, there was a tremendous change in her life. Not only was she happier, she also had a lot of positive opportunities open up to her.

Change is scary. There are so many unknowns. We hope for something or someone to make the changes for us so we don't have to make the decisions ourselves. What if I'm wrong? What if it's worse? What if I can't do this? What if I fail? What will people think? What will they say about me? These self-doubting questions can go on and on. If someone else or some outside influence makes the choice for us, we can blame the outcome on them when things go wrong.

The problem with that is it leads to a victim mindset, which makes you lose control over your life. Everything that happens in your life happens *to* you instead of *for* you. When you look at it as though things happen *to* you, it allows you to play the victim role. You aren't a willing participant. Instead, you are just a member of the audience watching your life. It is super easy to be a victim and our culture loves them. Victims get sympathy, attention, and support. An example would be when someone goes on a weight loss program and they say, "*I can't eat that dessert.* It isn't on my diet." People quickly rush in to comfort and say, "Oh, poor you. Diets are so hard. You must be suffering all the time. What else won't they let you eat? Are you sure you don't want a taste? Things will be so much better when you're off that diet." Just by the wording of *can't*, you have become a victim to your program. Mind you, you chose to be on that program and know that if you lose the weight, not only will you feel better and lengthen your life, but you'll also be able to avoid the type two diabetes drugs your doctor wants to put you on.

When you say can't, you can feel the

negativity in your body. Your shoulders drop a little, you tend to frown, and feel like a weight has been placed on you. Playing a victim is not only hard mentally it is hard physically. As I explained from my own personal experience, years of living this way take its toll. The worst part is that it is fear-based living. *Playing a victim prevents you from living the life you want.*

Empowerment

When we take responsibility for every single aspect of our lives, we become immensely empowered. We have the choice to make our lives what we want them to be. You aren't waiting on someone else to help you. As we all know, you could be waiting a long time or forever. No one knows what you want unless you tell him or her. We often feel alone in our situations. - No one could possibly understand what I'm going through and why I'm like this. No one loves or cares for me. – Again, this is victim mindset. Feeling alone is a very common problem, and a top reason why people are on anti-depressants. Once you get into this mindset, it is a downward spiral.

As we make decisions for ourselves, things begin to miraculously align to help us reach our goals and wants. Have you ever had a close friend start his or her own business? Wouldn't you just help them out with it by telling all your friends about it because you are so excited for them and know this is something they have been working hard on and want? They don't even have to ask you to. You just do it because you want to. When people shoot for the things they want, the universe is there to support it. Communities will come together to help.

Let's go back to the example of the weight loss program. Reframing the above situation, instead of saying I *can't* eat that dessert, a better response would be- I *choose* not to eat that dessert. - Try that out. When you say I choose, you can feel yourself straighten up a bit, your voice becomes stronger, and you feel more positive. How could you not feel that way? You have taken control of the situation and made a decision that aligns with your health and goals. That feels a lot better than someone patting you on the back and saying, Poor you, eat the piece of cake. The victim mindset seems like the better way and is how most of us live our lives. However, taking responsibility is truly the way to design the life you want and to gain strength to make it happen.

In the next exercise, you will explore the ways you are playing the victim in your life and how to turn it around to be empowered.

Exercise:

Time to grab the journal again and find a comfortable place to sit. Quiet the mind and come into the present by taking several breaths through your nose and exhaling through your mouth. Open the journal and think about your day. Do you recall any time you complained about something or were accusatory toward someone? These are situations in which you play the victim. On the left hand page, write down as many examples from the day as you can recall in which you played the victim. Do this without judging yourself. Now, on the right hand page, write down how you could have taken responsibility for the situation. This part will be much harder. However, with practice, it becomes easier. Some examples are –

- You have a conversation with a friend and tell them about how unfairly you're being treated at work. Your boss is always giving you a hard time and making your life hell.

  An example of taking responsibility in the boss situation, might be saying – I don't really like my job, so everything my boss does annoys me because I don't want to be in the office.

- You find yourself saying, "I am the only one in this house who does the laundry and cleans. No one ever helps."

  Taking responsibility might be saying – I never ask for help when it is time to do the laundry so my family can see what a sacrifice I make to take care of them.

It is a bit surprising, huh? Once you start to

become aware of how you play the victim, it becomes easier and easier to see it in yourself and the people around you. Once we become aware of a behavior, we can then make a change when we recognize we are doing it. Note that the key is not to judge yourself. Judging brings you back to a negative state. As you become aware of it, you will start to do it less and less and consider ways you might have reacted differently. It takes time to change habits. Play with it.

∂∾∾

Although we know we want and need change, we can sometimes get confused about what that means to us and what we really want. This can lead to feeling overwhelmed and becoming stuck in our thought process. When you went through the clutter, you started to physically clear areas within your environment. As you did that, you were able to see the room better and in its entirety, not just focusing on one cluttered spot. You started to make decisions on what served you and what you thought was ugly or unnecessary in your life. You were able to do this because you started to move things around and changed the energy in the room. The hardest part is starting, and then the momentum takes on. Once the energy was moving, it brought clarity into the environment and showed you what other areas needed attention. Just like you've cleared your space of clutter, you now have the tools to clear your mind of those things that don't serve you. Think of clutter as the victim mindset. Once your mind is free from mental clutter, you can begin to see things more clearly and act with fearlessness and beauty.

Fourteen

Creating A Calm

& Inspiring Home

You have done the work to clear the physical and mental clutter around you and allow the stagnant energy to flow in positive manner. You have also agreed to allow beauty into your life to support you with your journey and to help you shine in the most positive and powerful way within your environment. The next step is to surround yourself with beauty.

In the previous chapters, we've discussed how clutter brings a sense of ugliness. Clutter creates chaos, busyness, and distraction. It keeps us from living up to our true and powerful potential. Clutter reflects that we are living in a negative and self-repressed state. When you are in a beautiful, clutter-free environment there is a sense of warmth, harmony, and balance. You can feel a sense of expansiveness and positivity. With beauty comes potential, inspiration and all things needed to support you to become more successful.

Are you ready to bring in some elements of beauty into your life or enhance what you already have? The following guide provides simple ways to do so immediately. When I bring this up with clients, it often makes them nervous. They immediately ask, "What is this going to cost me? How much work am I going to have to do? Am I going to have to hire an interior designer?" The wonderful thing about this process is that you can make it what you want it to be. Just like in life, you decide what you want. It's part of being fearless. Listen to and trust the deep inner voice and you will understand just how much or little you need.

You have already accomplished step one by clearing clutter, which has made your area look better and helped you feel lighter and clearer. The next step is to clean your space.

Cleaning

As good as clearing clutter can feel, cleanliness is the icing on top. The problem with cleaning is that people have extreme emotional reactions to it. They hate it, love it, are indifferent to it, or obsessed with it. In any case, it's time to make peace with cleaning.

The Power of Cleaning

You know that saying "Cleanliness is next to Godliness?" When things are clean, there is a feeling of calm, peace, and the sublime. Dirt, grime and dust distract, multiply, cause stagnation, and create negativity. Clutter attracts and holds filth. With the clutter gone, you now have an opportunity to do a deep clean, which will literally sweep up the negative energy and send it on its way. By moving things around, removing objects, clearing space, you are able to get into areas that you probably haven't seen in a while. Undoubtedly, these areas have collected dust bunnies and dead bugs.

How Disorder Holds You Back

If you are embarrassed to have people over to your house, usually the biggest reason is that you're embarrassed that it is dirty and disorderly. When we neglect our homes, we neglect ourselves. When we take pride in our homes, we take pride in ourselves. Having a clean and well-cared-for home is honors you. Fearlessly welcoming people into your home is a way to give of yourself and share your life with others. This is a beautiful way to live.

Make Peace With Cleaning

The thing about cleaning, like clutter, is it can cause a lot of arguments between family and friends. One person is ambivalent to it while for another it is important.

Understand Your Relationship With Cleaning

Most people who are ambivalent to cleaning have no interest because they do not want to do the work. When we do not take care of our environments, it reflects what little care and respect we have for ourselves.

163

People can also use cleaning to play the victim. They get into the role of saying, "I am the only one who cleans; look what I sacrifice in order to make sure the house is clean; I spend hours doing this for you." If you decided to clean, it should come from a place of love. A healthier way to look at cleaning is to ask yourself, "what do *I* get out of it when I spend my time cleaning?" Then, look at it from a place of gratitude and list the ways it enhances your life, such as creating a beautiful space to welcome the people you love.

On the extreme side, people become obsessed with cleaning because it makes them feel like they have control over something in their lives. They use it as a way to also control the other people in their environments. They will spend hours cleaning to avoid social situations, enjoying their lives ,and spend time with their loved ones. If you use cleaning in any of these ways, part of becoming fearless is to change your relationship with the process. A healthier approach is to ask yourself, "What am I lacking in my life and what can I do to feel empowered in this situation?" By asking questions like this, you take control over making positive changes in your life versus feeling overwhelmed and lonely via cleaning obsession.

The Cleanliness Solution

One of the best ways to solve the cleanliness dilemma is to hire a house cleaner. No joke. Almost everyone I work with complains that they spend too much time cleaning. Things get messy. There is no avoiding it. Add in a partner, children and pets, and there is definitely no getting around that things will have to be cleaned and washed regularly. Is there any wonder that, for most of human existence, there has been an occupation of being a housewife?

There is a lot that needs to happen to keep a house and asking for help is ok. If your family or housemates are unwilling to pitch in, then it is time to hire outside help. I get the most resistance with this from clients. It brings up all sorts of "I'm-no-good" feelings. Overachievers want to be able to handle everything. There is tremendous guilt that comes from the perception of not being able to handle something--especially when that something is associated with creating a home and family. Anyone who had a mother growing up who took care of everything and always kept a neat house is especially susceptible to this.

The thing is, times have changed. Free time is now more precious as our society continually speeds up with technology and endless personal and professional obligations. did your mother answer emails and phone calls through the night when she got home from work? Did she continue that work on the weekends? Did she commute hours per week for work? Probably not.

Hiring a house cleaner was life changing to me. My partner and I kept a clean house, but I always felt I did all the cleaning. I traveled heavily for work at the time and was home only on the weekends. Admittedly I took on the victim role, and spent my Saturday mornings cleaning and being bitter that I had to do it during the only free time I had. One particular Saturday, I had really worked myself into a frenzy of resentment that I had to clean; I felt guilt that I couldn't seem to take as good care of my house as my mother; and angry at my partner for not helping me although I never asked him to. As I vacuumed, I grew angrier and angrier, paying little attention to my surroundings. And then it happened: I slipped on the stairs. As I rolled down the stairs yelling, I grabbed a banister, which broke in my hand.

The universe sends us a sign when we need it.

My partner stood at the top of the stairs looking down at me. After learning that I wasn't dead or had any broken bones, he loudly proclaimed, "Annick! That's it! We're getting a house cleaner whatever the cost."

It was one of the best decisions we ever made. Actually, it was the best decision my partner ever made. At that time, I never would have done it on my own without his prompting. But before I hired someone, I had two concerns about hiring someone.

First, I felt guilty because it seemed like I was letting my mother down, and that she would think it was a waste of money. Whoa. Where did that come from? It certainly didn't come from my mother because I had never even talked to her about it. It came from not feeling good enough, which was my own issue and had nothing to do with her. I know she loves me and would only want the best for me. If I thought hiring someone would help me, I'm sure she would support that. And, as an adult not living in her home, it's none of her business. It's *my* business and I made up this whole story in my head that never existed. What a waste of time, energy and emotion.

My second concern was that whomever we hired wouldn't do as good of a job as me. Hello, perfectionist! When you are scared of something, you bring it in. The person we hired isn't as good as me, but it didn't matter. They do a really good job and that is good enough. What I'm nitpicking at is so minor that if it bothers me, it only takes 10 minutes for me to clean versus the hours I had originally spent.

The first objection clients usually have when I suggest they hire a house cleaner is that it's too expensive. This is what I tell them. Multiply how much money you make per hour by how many hours it takes for you to thoroughly clean your home. Now, take into account that a professional, well-equipped house cleaner can usually clean an area three times faster than you. I guarantee you will pay a lot less for a house cleaner than you would pay yourself for doing the same job. If you are still reticent to the idea, hire someone to come once a month and decide from there how frequently you need them. Be sure to shop around, as prices vary greatly depending on where you live and what you need.

Help and Happiness

I get downright giddy when I come home after my cleaning lady has been in my home. Immediately when I walk through the door, I can feel the change in the house. It feels fresher and calmer. The energy is immediately lifted. Although it seems like a luxury, you should seriously consider hiring help if you work more than 35 hours a week. The money I spend ends up being an investment in myself. I can now spend those hours working on my business, making more money, being creative, or spending time with my loved ones. I may have spent hard-earned money on the service, but I've *gained* hours in my week. The best part is that my home sparkles and looks absolutely beautiful when it's clean.

Furniture Arrangement

How a room is set up has a lot to do with how comfortable someone feels in it. There are a lot of interior design tricks to make the layout of furniture more inviting. And you don't need to be a professional to arrange a room. You are going to tap into your intuition to achieve the same effect.

Furniture Arrangement Basics

There are basic elements that make rooms function better. For example, there should always be a comfortable place to sit, varied lighting, and a table or furniture to put things on. This can be applied in any room of a house. Since you've cleared out your clutter, you can now look at a room more objectively. If you feel the slightest bit uneasy, something needs to be changed.

Embrace Change

Keep in mind that just because you have always lived with furniture in a certain way doesn't mean you have to keep it that way. I have changed the arrangement of my living room every single year. Some rooms don't need to be touched, but my living room sees the most traffic and evolves constantly--like my life. By changing it around, the energy changes. New furniture and pieces come in and out. What worked for a year may no longer work. As soon as I sit down and feel the slightest bit uncomfortable in the room, I know it's time to change the setting.

Before you begin to arrange a room, ask your self the following questions about how you'd like it to be used:

• Is it a public or private place?

- Do you want people to be in it with you or do you want to be alone?
- How do you want the room to feel?
- Do you want it to be calm, lively, a place for laughter or a place for quiet and reflection?

How you group your furniture will do a lot to set the tone of the room. The best way to intuitively arrange your room for what you need is to roll up your sleeves and start moving furniture around.

At first, you may feel frustrated because every way you move the furniture around doesn't feel comfortable. If so, take a break and bring someone else into the room. Ask them how they feel. With an open mind and heart, listen to what they have to say and see if, together, you can come up with a better arrangement. Perhaps some piece of furniture needs to leave the room to open up the right arrangement. Or maybe you need a new piece to replace something that isn't working. Be fearless and explore all options until you feel satisfied that you have a setting that feels comfortable and reflects what you want for the room. Believe your intuition--you have the answer inside you.

Bedrooms

It is incredibly important to your health and wellbeing to get 7 to 8 hours of sleep each night. While this is a known fact, many people struggle to sleep through the entire night. A lot of that has to do with how a bedroom is set up.

You have already cleared the clutter out of your bedroom so there should be as few pieces of furniture as you need there. The more visual stimulants you have in the bedroom, the more active your mind will be, which will make it harder to have a sound night's sleep. On the contrary, a lot of *open space* helps create a serene environment. It's also important how the bedroom functions. It's best to use it to sleep and make love only. Avoid using it as an office, if possible. Make sure closet doors and dresser drawers are closed at all times.

Do not eat in your bed. Kitchens are meant for eating. Bedrooms are made for sleeping. When you leave crumbs and dirty your bed, you void your sacred area. Your bed should reflect how you want to be treated.

Build a Better Bed

Spend as much money as you can afford on a mattress. There is no other piece of furniture we use as much as our beds and it is usually the one piece we skimp out on because no one sees it. Beds--aside from our desks--are also the one piece of furniture that can cause the most physical pain. Lumpy, poorly made mattresses can lead to back, neck and hip issues--among others--and can make it difficult for you to sleep comfortably. With a mattress, you get what you pay for. Set a budget and know that for the next 7 years you will spend an average of 17,885 hours in it. That's more time than you spend in your car. I also suggest buying the best quality sheets as you can. Look for natural fibers, like cotton or linen that allows your skin to breathe. Avoid polyester whenever possible. This will help with your overall health.

In addition, change your pillows every 2 to 3 years. Ever notice how light new pillows feel? Pillows harbor dust mites and germs, which, over time, weigh them down. Anything that you have near your face should be as clean and breathable as possible. Aside from your bathroom, your bed should be the most luxurious place in your house. There is a lot that happens to our bodies and minds while we sleep. Honoring that as a sacred space is very important. It reflects that you love and honor yourself.

Avoid Electronics

Keep the electronics out of the bedroom. Phones should be placed in another room while you sleep. That means, do not sleep with your phone beneath your pillow and use it as an alarm clock. In a study published by the Endocrine Society, it was found that watching brightly lit screens before bed can prevent you from falling asleep. These lights stimulating the mind and suppress the function of melatonin--a hormone needed to regulate your body's biorhythm--which will reduce sleep quality. TVs should also be removed from the bedrooms and placed in the public rooms like the den or living room.

Develop a Sleep Routine

Many people have difficulty falling asleep. However, developing a bedtime ritual can help tremendously. People forget that when they were babies or children, their parents usually put them through a bedtime ritual. It could have included a bath, bedtime story, saying prayers or having their backs rubbed. Just as those things put you to bed as a child, creating a similar ritual for yourself can help you to sleep deeply. For example, shut off the TV and other electronics a half hour to full hour before you go to bed. Then, dim the lights, and pick up a book to read or use your journal to write things down that you are grateful for from your day. Easing into sleep will help immensely.

Bathrooms

Bathing is a reflection of our self-care and worth. A bathroom that has a sense of luxury and efficiency will add more beauty to your life. Note that I use the word "luxury" as a *feeling*, not as a monetary value.

Fix the Problems

Frustration can occur in bathrooms when parts of it do not work appropriately. For example, leaky faucets, a runny toilet, or things that get knocked off counters and sinks need to be addressed. Remember, they are a reflection of your life. Bathrooms should function effortlessly. You should be able to step out of a shower and easily reach your towel. If this doesn't happen, rearrange the space or install a holder that's within arm's reach of the shower. Fix other issues by hiring a plumber, carpenter, or look online for DIY websites for tutorials. Though it will take concentration and practice, novices can fix most bathroom issues. Not only will you have fixed your bathroom issues, you'll gain life skills that you can use in other areas of your life.

Ritualize Bath Time

Just as you've developed bedtime rituals, you can bring more beauty into your life with bathing rituals. Here are suggestions to make bath time a luxurious and transformative experience:

- Use a body brush before you bathe. Your skin is your biggest organ and can use the love. Always brush towards your heart.
- If you have a bathtub, use it. Taking, at the very least, a 15-minute bath

once a month can do a world of
wonders for your stress levels.

- Take a hot bath with Epsom salts to
soothe muscles and relax the mind.
- Before taking a bath, light candles and
set an intention. Bring yourself fully
into the present and say out loud
one thing you are grateful for.
- Use towels that are fluffy, clean, and
do not have holes or tears in them.
Honor your body by using materials
that feel good against your skin.
Choose colors and patterns that lift
your spirit and feel super fresh.

Kitchens

Where you prepare and eat your food is the heart
of your home. Food nourishes your body, mind,
and soul. It is important to be sensitive to this
environment. Your kitchen should be a room that
you enjoy spending time in, can navigate easily,
and has space for more than one person, unless
you live in a micro apartment in a city.

Build a Navigable Space

Have you ever been to a dinner or house party only to find that the attendees spend most of the time in the kitchen? People *love* to gather in kitchens. You should be able to move around your kitchen and cook efficiently. If it doesn't feel right, reorganize your dishes, appliances, and utensils. Label your food and spices. Everything should have a designated place and be as organized as possible. Like the bathroom, ensure everything is in working order. All doors and drawers should be closed when not in use. As an added note, chances are you'll be more likely to cook fresh, healthy, homemade meals if your kitchen has enough space for another person.

Beautify Your Refrigerator

Focus on making your refrigerator pretty. A lot of people will tack pictures, clippings, and stuff onto their fridge door. Take it off. All this stuff is clutter and will hide issues around food. By having a clear surface, you honor the food contained within the refrigerator. Keep the inside of your refrigerator clean and organized. Go through it daily and get rid of all things that are expired. Use matching containers to put food in--preferably glass ones instead of plastic. When your fridge is attractive and inviting you'll eat better and take more care with the preparation of your food.

Address Your Tableware

Consider your dishes, glassware, and flatware. You should love the pattern, style, weight, and feel of what you use. If these items annoy you or cause distress, you will swallow your Caesar salad with a side of anxiety. Eating should be enjoyable and having the right tableware can enhance the experience. Oh yeah, and give up those paper dishes and plastic cups and use real dishes for a week. I promise you will enjoy your meals more.

Be Mindful

Give grace or an intention. When you pause before your meal, you honor the work you have done to prepare it, what you are eating and how it will nourish your body. You don't necessarily have to say a prayer; acknowledging what you have before you brings your attention to the present and makes you aware of your surroundings and intent. We digest our food better when we eat mindfully;

mindful eating cuts down on bloating, indigestion, and overindulging. Mindfulness is the most respect you can bring to yourself and the people dining with you.

Lighting

Window Treatments

Lighting can set a mood in your home. Attention to lighting can foster positive energy, improve productivity, and enhance sleep quality. In most rooms, it's ideal to allow as much natural light in as possible. However, if you feel vulnerable or uncomfortable in a room--there's too much visual access into your home from a nearby street or pathway--use window treatments to obscure that access and create some privacy. Part of creating a beautiful home is to feel safe within it; window treatments can help enhance feelings of safety. Alternately, in bedrooms, use window treatments that darken the space as much as possible. Excess light can result in poor sleep quality.

Overhead Lighting

Rooms in which you work or spend a lot of time--such as kitchens--should have strong overhead lighting. It can be frustrating when you're trying to finish a task and you cannot see what you are doing. Poor lighting dulls your senses and keeps you from doing your best work. I recommend LED bulbs for kitchens to bring in the best and most efficient light possible. While still pricy at this point, they are well worth the investment.

Mood Lighting

The third type of light a room should have is what I call mood lighting, which is a secondary source that is soft and indirect. These lights are used to bring a feeling of relaxation to the room. For example, place lamps or pendants that bring light to smaller spots in gathering areas.

Candlelight

The fourth type of light is a candle. Candles bring a special sense of calmness and purpose to a room. Use them with your bed and bath time rituals and while setting intentions. Use them to play with scents and see which smells reflect the right mood for you. Candles can create a beautiful and powerful atmosphere, but always exercise caution while using them as they can pose a risk to your safety if left unattended.

Flowers & Plants

An easy way to brighten and enliven a room is to fill it with fresh flowers. Nature is amazing and endless in its beauty. We spend so much time indoors that bringing some of the outdoors in can be refreshing and uplifting. It is also a wonderful way to change the colors in a room without painting or buying new pillows. Cut some flowers and branches or decorative grasses from your yard and use them to make your own bouquets. Or purchase some from the local grocery store during your weekly shopping trip.

Plants also create a healthy and positive environment. Not only do they purify the internal air, they also add a spot of life in a room. There are plenty that need very little maintenance and watering and any nursery can advise you on what will work for your home and lifestyle. The nice thing about a plant is, if you kill it, you can just throw it in the compost pile and start over. There is no loss as they get recycled back to earth.

Art & Objects

Art and other decorative items can enhance the beauty of a home, but be selective in what you choose; art can either enhance a home or make it a cumbersome place to live.

We have a tendency to pick art based on a particular emotion or interest, which can be a wonderful and a beautiful representation of your personality. However, it can also send the wrong message. For example, a handsomely photographed desolate landscape might catch your eye, but you may give the wrong impression if your goal is to be surrounded by a warm and loving family. The artwork in that case is not a reflection of your desires. Instead, it's a repellant to the very things you say you want in your life.

When you have chosen items that reflect your interests and personality, be sure to hang them in groupings versus having one piece that is alone and hung too high. The solo image will often seem out of place and may also reflect feelings of loneliness. Art that is hung in groupings creates more balance and relationship between the pieces. This will also be reflected into the area.

Collections of objects should be continually evaluated and gone through to avoid any obsessive behavior. Fixating on one particular thing can be good when we want to achieve a goal in life. However, it can also work against us if the focus becomes so singular that it blocks other ideas, experiences and opportunities from entering our lives.

When choosing art and objects, consider how it makes you feel in the moment and if this were how you would like to feel everyday. Be aware of the colors and texture. Are they in line with what you want for yourself? Take the color yellow, for example. Yellow is known to be a cheerful and inspiring color. It is associated with spirituality, creativity, clarity and positive thinking. Yellow is used to engage communication and is often used in rooms where people gather, such as kitchens. Color is a fascinating subject. For more in depth information, I suggest doing a search on the topics of color theory and color psychology.

Like color, texture also plays a role in how you feel within a room. If you have a living room where all the objects are hard--hardwood floor, stiff couch, glass figurines--you will feel rigid and cold yourself. Have you ever been inside a grandmother's formal living room and didn't want to sit down? However, if the same room is given a warm area rug, soft pillows for the sofa and decorated with some organic objects from nature like branches and flowers, the room immediately becomes inviting.

Special Areas

Workout Space

Most workout spaces in a home are used for a short amount of time and then neglected. To minimize neglect, create an area that inspires you to exercise. Here are some tips to make your workout space more appealing and inviting:

- Workout gear looks ugly when it is all jumbled together. Aim to keep this area clean.
- Choose equipment that you *like* to use. If you hate walking on a treadmill, don't buy one for your house.

- Donate equipment if you lose interest in it, otherwise, the sight of the pieces you hate will negatively impact your motivation to exercise.

- Most equipment comes in black or grey. Many smaller gym pieces--like exercise balls, yoga mats, and bands--come in all sorts of colors and patterns. Find ones that you love the look of. The visual splash will encourage you to use them. It will also make the area look livelier and enticing, instead of some dark dusty punishing spot.

Meditation Space

Meditation has proven to increase feelings of wellbeing and happiness into the lives of people who practice it. Dedicate a quiet, peaceful and serene space for your meditation practice. This area can be as simple or involved as you like. Some people meditate seated in an area of the home that they feel is peaceful, such as a favorite chair or a place by a window with a special view. If you choose to practice on a mediation cushion, be mindful to keep the area free of clutter. The cushion should have a little bit of space around it and placed in a quiet area of the home. Choose a cushion that you love and that makes you feel good. If you use incense or candles, select those with calm, uplifting smells and colors.

Altar

Many cultures and religions will keep an altar within the home. An altar is a place to honor Divine energies, express gratitude, give offerings and ask for blessings and protection. Alters should be placed with consideration. Walk through the home and find an area that feels safe and honorable. If you are not aligned with a particular affiliation, you can also use an altar for your daily intentions. Your altar can be as simple as a plate and a candle. Altars are designed to bring awareness and purpose to your thoughts while honoring your act. When you put one together, let your intuition guide you to gather what you need for it. There is no wrong or right way to create an altar.

꙳꙳

In a previous exercise from Chapter 10, you started to take a look at the environment around you and identified what you already have that is beautiful and what you are unhappy with. In this chapter, you learned of some ways to surround yourself with beauty. In the exercise below, you will combine what you discovered and learned so that you can start to transform your home into a reflection of your most inspired self.

Exercise:

Choose an area within your home that you wouldn't usually decide to sit and work in. Perhaps it is on your stairs, perched on your bathtub, or in your laundry room. The point is to change your perspective by changing your environment. Once you have chosen a spot and have made yourself comfortable, bring your attention to the present by taking several breaths in through your nose and out through your mouth.

Take out your journal and open it to the exercise from Chapter 10. Review what you wrote in the area that you found beautiful. Then write freely on the following questions:

- How can you make the area you do not like, more beautiful?
- Are there things you can move from the area you love to the area you hate to change it?
- What would it take for you to love and feel inspired in that area?

You don't need to spend a lot of money to transform your home into a beautiful and supportive environment. With clarity and intention, you can fearlessly create a home that reflects a life you have designed.

Fifteen

Creating A Productive Work Environment

We spend so much of our lives working, yet we seldom consider whether our work environment supports us to be more efficient and creative. We often just accept the cubicle or the workspace we have been given and then struggle to make it work. Unfortunately, this comes at a price. Without being aware of it, working in an environment that doesn't reflect beauty can dampen the ability to generate quality output. In a previous chapter, we discussed feelings of negativity while at work. In some cases, unhappiness at work can stem from your workspace. Wouldn't it be nice to love where you physically work? Whether you work in an office, cubicle or from home, this chapter will explain how to set up a space that honors your spirit and improves productivity.

Assess Your Space, Improve Your Productivity

If work feel stagnant and ideas are not coming easily, sometimes a change in environment may be what is needed to shake those creative juices loose. It is also a good indication that your current environment is in need of a change.

So, how does that work?

When I decided to write this book, I worked in a home office I had set up on the first floor of my townhouse. While the office is well organized with plenty of space, beautiful and functional furniture, and inspiring images, it didn't feel right. The first floor of the townhouse is a little on the dark side due to the location of the windows and the shade from nearby. I first chose this area because it is incredibly cozy and separated from the rest of the house, which allows me to focus and get work done. But, it always remains on the cool side because the floor is built on a slab of concrete and covered with ceramic tile.

Despite my love for the room, the ideas I had brewing for this project needed a more expansive space and light. Also, I did not want to be influenced or distracted by my other day-to-day work. As a special project, I aimed to give it the attention and dedication it needed to develop. I wanted to ensure that I was creatively inspired and able to make the best book I was capable of. Once I realized my current office would not work for this project; I considered attending a writing retreat, but quickly dismissed it. The number one reason I dismissed the idea is that this book is about how a person's environment is a reflection of herself. What does it say about me if I want to leave my own house to go write? The second reason was if I did go on the weeklong retreat, what happens if I don't finish the book during that time and I come back to the environment I'm not happy with? I'd still be in the same place I was when I started. After much consideration, I fearlessly decided that I could change my workspace in my own home and create a space that would inspire me to write a book.

New ideas can come in when we change our outlook and open ourselves to other possibilities. Since my current office works for my day-to-day work, I decided to set up a temporary desk in another part of my house. As I went through the different rooms and listened to my body in each one, I decided on the top floor because it felt right. It also happens to be my bedroom. I know, I told you to *avoid* doing anything but sleep and make love in the bedroom. Since this wasn't a permanent change, I wasn't too worried about disturbing that space with this project. I had also decided for the amount of time that I would spend on the book, I wanted to live, breathe, and sleep on it.

My next task was to set up the space and surround myself with beauty to accomplish my goals. I took out the folding card table from years ago and threw a brightly colored tablecloth over it. While the pattern isn't one that I would usually choose, I picked it for two reasons. First, I didn't want what I usually would do or choose because I wanted to take myself a little out of my comfort zone to see what would come of it. The second reason is that the pattern includes all my favorite colors and that makes me happy.

I then placed the table by the windows and decided to use one of my favorite orange midcentury modern chairs to sit in. I discovered the view from these windows was beautiful, which I never really noticed because I typically keep the curtains drawn for privacy. From a seated position, I was in the height of the trees and able to see the comings and goings of my neighbors. Watching them broke up the pauses when I contemplated how to phrase or structure a part of the book. The view felt expansive and the windows provided a ton of natural light, which made me feel invigorated and inspired.

In order to switch into the mindset of writing from my other work, I set up a mini altar on my writing table. Physically entering the room started to set the tone that I was undertaking a new task--rituals are also effective for work projects--but I still needed to bring my focus to the writing and not get distracted by the errands I needed to run, people I should call, or stories in my head. On my table, I set up a prayer flag I had sewn and beaded years ago. On top of it was a dish that I liked the design of which held some personally meaningful candles and stones I had picked up over time. It was a very simple and uncluttered grouping. Before I sat down to write, I would light a candle and proclaim my intention for the session. This simple act brought me into the present and focused my mind and energy on the task at hand. This process helped me get a lot of work done in a concentrated amount of time. It also made me very clear on why I was doing what I was doing. Setting an intention reinforces the notion that what you put out in the world comes back to you.

◈◈◈

Are you ready to set up an area to serve as your workspace to support the best work you are capable of? The following section features suggestions on how to create an office that is surrounded with beauty and a reflection of your fearless and highly successful self.

Cubicle & Office Spaces

Organize

While you may face restrictions on what you are allowed to do with your office or cubicle due to company policy, it is worth the time to set it up to make it as clutter free and productive as possible. The first step is to eliminate unnecessary papers and tradeshow tchotchkes, and clean your files. Work desks can become dumping grounds for a whole office of people. While you cannot control what your coworkers do with their areas, just focus on your own space and set it up to your liking.

Electronic Management

Next, get all your electronics in order. Make sure your computer and screens are set to the proper heights and are tilted to minimize strain on your body. Organize all the wires on and under the desk, which are oftentimes jumbled and chaotic. Create a sense of calm and order by bundling them in a solid, organized fashion.

Pick the Perfect Mouse

If you use a mouse with your computer, make sure you like it and that it works for you. If you don't like it, ask management for an option that better fits your needs. If they deny your request, purchase one yourself. While it may seem as though your company is obligated to provide you with the best possible working tools, they're not. Investing in a quality mouse can save you money in the long run and minimize the potential for aches, pains and injury. Also, you can take it with you if you chose to leave in the future. Having a mouse that you enjoy the look of and like to use can infinitely increase your happiness and ease at work. You won't waste time being distracted by messing with a mouse that doesn't work. That will enable you do get work done faster and get you out the door faster at the end of the day to pursue your other passions. All these little wins can add up throughout a day. Plus, this type of action once again helps you escape the role of the victim and into a mindset of control.

Assess the Details

Pay attention to the details within your space. Avoid excessive personal photos and images of your family and pets. Save them for your home office. At work, you want to keep a professional focus. Vision boards and inspiring images are helpful to keep in view, but there is no need to cover all your walls with them. The less visual distractions you have, the better. There are enough distractions within a work environment--colleagues dropping by to chat, meetings, emails, and phone calls. When your walls are pared down and clean, you will be better able to focus on the project at hand. With clarity, the quality of your work will be better.

Keeping to the essentials within the workspace creates breathable and moveable space within your area. It is hard to think of big, innovative ideas when you feel constricted. While having the minimal amount of stuff within your area, choose what you use judiciously. If you don't love how something looks or feels in your hands, replace it. This goes for pens, pads of paper, mouse pads, coffee mugs, etc. Small annoyances lead to grumpy moods, and at work it benefits you and the people around you to be content and happy with your workspace. This will put you in a better mood and people will be attracted to you because of your personality, which may open up doors for you that you have never imagined.

It's important to note that you *can* create the work environment that you want. If you already love the company you work for, where you work, or if this is your own business, rearranging your workspace will allow you to do work in even greater alignment with your goals and aspirations. Surrounding yourself with beauty and productivity will increase your energy and give the opportunity for creative ideas to come into your life. This will, in turn, make you even more successful.

If you feel uninspired and that you are spinning your wheels at work or you just flat out hate your job, keep in mind that you have the power and control to change your situation and environment. By cleaning and rearranging your workspace, you will move stagnant energy and cause other changes to occur. At the very least, you will feel accomplished in that you have created a space that you enjoy being in. This will lead to better productivity and fresh ideas--perhaps ones that will get you out of that job.

Home Office

Apply the same basic guidelines to your home office as described in the previous section. Make sure that your office functions effortlessly. Your computer, screen, mouse and chair should all be set up in a way that causes you the least amount of pain and strain. I'll leave it to you to research on the Internet how to adjust the ergonomics of your seated position to be in an optimal position for using a computer. This will do a lot for the health of your body.

Your Office, Personally

The biggest difference between work and home is personality. At home, you have carte blanche to set up your office in any style that you want. If you want all your accessories to be in zebra print or your favorite football team's colors, have at it. One of the challenges may be to figure out how to set up your office if you have to share the space with other people in the household. First, I recommend making sure you have your own desk. You need a space that belongs only to you and has only your things in it. Once other people's things encroach on your workspace, it can wreak havoc on your productivity and concentration. You'll spend unneeded time trying to get rid of it and it will bring up a lot of useless emotions. Instead, by having your own space, you will be able to focus on your tasks and goals at hand. Your work becomes about you and will not be sidetracked by outside influences.

Make sure to surround yourself with accessories that you love and make your life simpler. If the old printer is finicky and you have never been able to get it to work properly, donate it and get a new one. Everything in your office should serve to make your life easier. If you experience difficulty setting up your electronics, hire a company to take care of the dirty work. Like hiring a house cleaner, some things are better left in the hands of professionals. You have more important things to do than get sidetracked working on a project outside your skillset.

Decorate Purposefully

Surround yourself with beautiful and inspiring images and objects, but not too much so that they over shadow *your* presence in the room. A few choice images can go a long way. You don't need to fill a wall with random, chaotic items. Update the images and vision boards yearly or as frequently as needed to make sure that they are relevant to where you are currently in your life. The same goes for the objects you choose to put on your desk. Make sure that all artwork supports what you want in your life. Beware of hanging any negative or depressing art. This can drag down your energy and cause you to become lethargic and stagnant.

Furnish Wisely

Choose furniture that you love and that fits you. If you inherited your grandfather's desk, but find it too large and cumbersome in your chosen space, let it go. It is ok; you will be able to find a worthy home for it. A lot of older desks do not fit the needs of the digital era, anyway. If you love your ergonomic chair, but it doesn't fit with the old desk, replace it with one that allows the arm rests to fit under the desk surface. When these small details work, other small things will begin to work in your life. You don't have to work around problems when you have the power to solve them yourself. *You have the ability to make the changes that will make your environment reflect your most capable and creative self.*

Store Intelligently

Storage within an office can be tricky. However, it should be somewhat easier now that you have accomplished the difficult task of getting rid of office clutter. All that is left should be things that you definitely need and like for your day-to-day work. There is no need to keep anything "just in case" because the future will provide for you in ways that you can't imagine. When you do need to store your papers and things for work, choose matching storage options like folders and containers. Having the same color within an area or similar sizes in boxes will cut down on the visual clutter. If you have lots of different sized boxes, colors and patterns, it becomes a visual jumble that makes the room's energy frenetic. It can be hard to get a lot of quality work done in that kind of space.

Add Life

Bring a fresh element into the home office like flowers or a plant. The beauty of the living thing will not only inspire you, it will also improve the quality of the air you breathe.

Now that you have surrounded yourself with beauty, bring intention to your work. Light a candle or some incense and bring your focus to the work you want to accomplish. Fearlessly say out loud what you would like to achieve. It can be anything from finishing x, y or z today to positively affecting one person in the world with your work. When you are clear about what you want, you have a greater ability to make it happen.

ॐ

In this last exercise, you will formulate what you would like to accomplish in your work and life, and you will create a plan to make it happen.

Exercise:

As you work on aligning your environment to be a reflection of your best self, it is now time to get clear on what you want to accomplish with your life. Deep down, you know the answer to this. Sometimes it gets all jumbled up with the outside noise and stories in our heads. Find a quiet spot in your home. Take out your journal and open to a fresh page. On the left side, write five things you would like to accomplish in the next year. Don't over-think it; just jot down what first comes to mind, even if it feels outlandish or trite. For each of the five goals, write down how you would feel if you accomplished the goal. What would it look and feel like to you if you were in the present with the goal having been met? Get as descriptive as you can with each goal. What would you be wearing? Would anyone be with you? Etc. Beside each of the five goals, write down three things it would take, action-wise, to accomplish the goal.

Our goals are a lot more manageable when we can envision them happening. They don't seem like these aimless dreams or wants floating around in our heads. When we think about how we can actually accomplish the goals, it gives us a solid course of action we can follow to make it happen. It gives us clarity on what we want and what we are working toward. A productive work environment supports this process and makes it easier to achieve goals by giving us the physical tools we need to make it happen.

ॐॐ

It's possible for all of us to create a productive work environment filled with beauty, even when restricted by company policy. It doesn't take much to make it happen except the willingness to make a change and belief that it is possible. When you design a workspace that you love, you can create work that aligns with your highest ideas and aspirations. When you take control of your environment and develop a space that reflects your current achievements and desired accomplishments, you allow yourself to fearlessly attain what is most important to you.

Conclusion

Your surroundings are a reflection of your life.

When I finished writing *Clear*, I took an hour and rearranged my living room while I was on a conference call. Thank goodness for mute! I knew I needed a change after putting forth a huge creative effort. The finished book signified a new chapter in my life. My current living room, all of a sudden, didn't support that new chapter and felt small. As I rearranged, organized and threw out a few things, I felt better and better. At the end of the conference call, one of the participants remarked, "Annick, you are really in a good mood today." As I sat back on the black Eames sofa and kicked my feet up onto the coffee table, I responded, "Yes, I most certainly am!" I was very

207

satisfied with the new layout, which felt expansive and fresh. I knew it aligned with how excited I felt to have completed *Clear* and to share it with the world. I was also ready to embrace a fresh, post book, chapter in my life.

છે∽છ

When you clear your clutter and simplify the way you live, you allow clarity to enter into your life. *Clear* is designed to help you align your environment to what you want out of life so that you can be more successful, live fearlessly and surround yourself with beauty. It is an empowering way to live.

Deep down, you know what does and does not serve you. The exercises in *Clear* help you tap into that intuition so you can make decisions that enhance the quality of your life and support success in reaching your goals.

Above all, remember to have fun with this process. It is incredibly rewarding to design a life that allows you to shine from within your surroundings and reflect your healthiest vibrant self. Now, go play.

CLEAR

Acknowledgements

First off, a major thank you to my readers! Without you, there would be no book to write. The experiences that you share with me keep me endlessly inspired to continue my quest to be a better person, writer, coach, and designer.

I thank ma famille for your endless support when I present you with ideas and things I want to do. Your willingness to drop what you're doing to drive hours to help me out exemplifies your love and does not go unnoticed. I love you.

My Love: Thank you for your support and understanding when I need to get things done. Your fortitude inspires me daily. You keep me sharp and full of love.

To the best Editor a lady can ask for: Ryan, thank you for making the process easy and intuitively understanding what I want to say. You make me a better writer and I look forward to working on future projects together.

For the two strangers at that fancy bar in Nashville, TN: Thank you for listening to me talk about the book I planned to write and encouraging me to pursue my dreams. Our conversation is exactly what I needed on that day to get to where I am right now.

ANNICK MAGAC

About the Author

Award-winning furniture designer and Health Coach, Annick Magac has dedicated her life to helping people become more successful by overcoming fear-based thoughts and developing healthy surroundings filled with beauty. She often travels for work or pleasure; spending a lot of time in airplanes, cars and on motorcycles. In the rare moment that she is in one place for any length of time, you'll find her training in a gym, visiting a museum, or immersed in a creative project.

Annick Magac is available for select readings and lectures. To inquire about a possible appearance, please contact info@annick-magac.com. Visit her website for one-on-one or group coaching and consultations at www.annick-magac.com.

Send Your Stories

*Has anything in this book
created a success in your life?*

Sharing your story inspires others to make changes in their lives. Have you transformed your home to be the center of love and laughter? Has clearing your kitchen allowed you to lose the weight you have been holding onto? Has getting rid of clutter helped you to make life-changing decisions? Write to Annick Magac with your success stories at the following email address.

clearbook@annick-magac.com

Include your written permission for Annick to publish your story if you are willing to share it with the world and inspire others.

Visit Annick's website at www.annick-magac.com to view stories that readers have submitted and for more information on all things related to health, mindset, and design.

Made in the USA
Middletown, DE
13 November 2014